# EMPOWERED
# FATHERING

# Empowered Fathering

*How to Navigate
Today's Fatherhood
Journey*

## ANDREW CHRIS, MS MFT

The Empowered Living Press

Empowered Fathering: How to Navigate Today's Fatherhood Journey

To my father, who taught me what it
means to be a dad - I love you Dad!

To my wife, for her tireless patience, love
and understanding - I wouldn't be a dad
without you!

To my children, who teach me everyday
about love and life!

# CONTENTS

# | 1 |

# Introduction

As a father, you have the power to change the world.

Now there's a bold claim! What do you think about that statement? Does it give you hope and energy to get out there and do your best? Or, does it make you feel pressured and a little bit stressed? That's how fatherhood goes sometimes, isn't it? One moment we feel charged and ready to go, and in the next, we feel like we don't know what we are doing. That is the journey of fatherhood!

Being a father is one of the most sacred titles we can hold. It comes with a ton of responsibility and has a tremendous impact on the world of our children. Unfortunately, fatherhood does not always get the respect and attention it deserves. It seems our society is frequently obsessed with where fathers fall short rather than where we excel.

Did you know that of all parents currently incarcerated, over 90% are fathers? How about the fact that one in two children grow up without their biological father? Are these scary statistics? Absolutely! Are they destiny? Absolutely not! The truth is when you look at the cultural story of fatherhood, we are up against some powerful forces. This is where we face a decision: we can be victims of these distorted views or be agents of change!

More fathers than ever are choosing to be agents of change. You are part of that wave of change. With each moment you spend with your child, mentoring them, and filling their life with love, you are changing the game. There is real power in being a father, and its influence spreads more sweeping than you can imagine. You can change the world, especially for your children. Are you ready for the next level?

## Time to Take the Challenge!

Fatherhood. Now there is a word that can throw your life for a complete loop! How different did you feel after you found out you were becoming a dad? Were you ready for the challenges that this role would bring? Let's face it, fatherhood is not the most effortless responsibility out there, even if it is incredible!

What makes being a dad so tricky? Is it the new responsibilities like changing a smelly diaper at 2 in the morning and then trying to set the child back in bed as gently as possible to keep a bomb from going off? Or, is it what we have to give up so that we can give to our children? There's nothing like replacing what you want to watch with Curious George or My Little Pony!

It doesn't get any easier as our children get older, does it? Instead of dealing with trying to get our children to eat their vegetables, we start dealing with complicated issues like drugs and underage drinking. Our mindset with a toddler is to hold them in our arms to keep them safe. As they grow older, we struggle with the challenge of opening our arms to give them the freedom they need to explore the world and who they want to become.

Fatherhood is a journey, not a list of tasks. This journey is full of ups and downs, highs and lows, and moments of triumph and others of uncertainty. Let's face it; we don't know everything we are taking on when we first become dads. Fatherhood also gets complicated because each child and the relationship you have with them will be its own unique journey. A lot is riding on our shoulders, and guess what, we can do this!

When it comes to this book, fathering is only part of the title. This book focuses on Empowered Fathering, which takes it to the next level! Empowered Fathering means having the knowledge and abilities you need to adapt and fulfill your role. This book's central tenet is that you will be the most effective father you can be when you know yourself.

Your most significant times of growth will come when you take those first difficult steps out of your comfort zone to stretch further than you ever have before. Personal trainers at gyms help push people beyond what they thought they could do by doing one more rep or adding more weight. This book is here to empower you to take that one extra step to reach a little further. Can you imagine how much growth will occur if you reach out just a bit further each day? You will see and feel it, and the bonus of that is so will your family!

Taking on fatherhood is not as easy as knowing $1+1=2$; instead, it feels more like a complicated calculus formula that only 12 people have figured out. I hope that this book will help you simplify the process a little bit. As an Empowered Father, you are being asked to draw on the strengths you already bring to the table. Fathering is a process, so there will always be room for growth and learning.

As you read through this book and find the things that speak to you, I encourage you to put what you learn into action. Without any action, nothing will change for you or your family. There will be things you have to take a chance and experiment with. The concepts in this book are meant to jive with your personality because if it isn't real to you, then it won't be genuine in your actions. The journey of fatherhood is yours; become what you choose to be!

While fatherhood is a journey, this book is not a map. It will not cover every situation you might face or what you should do in a given moment. Children do not come with a manual because each is so unique that a map could never do them justice. This book hopes to provide you with new tools and ways of looking at things so you can choose what should be done. Get to know yourself so you can see the uniqueness of your children. That way, you write your story together!

This book will help you grow into the man and father you want to be. The ideas and strategies come from the voices of hundreds of fathers I have worked with in different educational, professional, and therapeutic settings. As long as you are willing to give it a shot, there will be something in this book to learn to help you out, no matter where you are on your journey.

We are fathers, which puts us on a journey together. More is being asked of us than has ever been asked of dads before. This is not a journey where the end is reached in a few years or when you finish this book. You have to put in the time and effort to get through the struggle. Part of being an Empowered Father means looking at the long-term instead of just the short-term. You are fathering for the present and the future.

Sometimes life makes it hard to see beyond the moment you are in, which can get locked in your past. Hopefully, this book will challenge you to take a few extra steps so you can approach fathering in a new way. I am honored to be on this journey with you, and if you are ready to begin the Empowered Father journey, then let's do this together!

# | 2 |

# Our Family Background

Have you ever wondered why you father the way you do? Or why there are times you react, almost reflexively, and it catches you off guard with how automatic it was? How come you catch yourself saying things at times that remind you of something one of your parents would say? This has to happen for some reason, so where does it come from exactly?

As you take on your fatherhood journey, one thing that might become apparent to you is how the family you grew up in affects who you are as a dad today. Many of the ideas we will discuss in this book began to form when you were a child. Our early family experiences played a large part in shaping who we are and how we approach life. Before we move into this book's main concepts, it is worth taking a trip back in time to highlight the influence your childhood has on you as a dad.

As a young boy growing up, part of the way you view the world was shaped by the adults and family you had around you. This is especially true of the male role models you had. Some of us grew up with a calm and encouraging father, which may be part of your fathering today. Others have had a different experience, such as an abusive, controlling, or disconnected dad. Some have grown up without a dad at all. No matter what your experience was, it left an impression on you.

Was your father involved and a positive presence in your life? If that was the case, there is a good chance you want to be a similar dad for your children. While you will change some things and be the dad that fits your personality, chances are you feel you have a good starting foundation. This comes from the template you formed about fatherhood from your childhood and the positive experiences you had.

Did you have a present father, but he was not close to your ideal of what a dad should be? How might this still be influencing the dad you are today? Your fatherhood template may be made up of ideas and expectations that are the opposite of what your dad did. You may not want to repeat your dad's choices and mistakes, so you are striving hard to be different. These past experiences with your dad are still influencing who you are today.

If your father was absent, how has he still impacted who you are as a dad today? Can having a childhood without positive memories of your father still influence who you are as a dad? The answer is, of course, yes. Have you noticed a drive to be present with your children as much as possible? Do you feel a deep desire to do whatever you can to help your children grow and have an awesome life? Your father's absence is likely a huge motivational force behind your goals for yourself as a dad today.

One of the nice things about life is there is variety, and this applies to father-figures. Other males who might have played a role in helping you develop a fatherhood template are uncles, grandpas, brothers, teachers, coaches, or mentors. Men in these types of roles taught you about masculinity and how to care for others. Your template will include ideas you gathered from this different group of men as well.

When you start to highlight those who influenced you throughout your life, you come to a better understanding of yourself. The more you know yourself and what you will do, the less likely you will repeat parts of your life you don't want to. When a person *reacts* to a situation, they will turn to old habits and patterns of behavior. The more you know yourself, the more you will know what you will do. Let's see what else we can learn while we are still time traveling to the past.

## Our Family of Origin

What did the family you grew up in look like? How many parents were in the home? Were there any grandparents? How many siblings did you have, and where did you fall in the birth order? Your family of origin is the family you grew up in as a child, and you all had a powerful influence on one another. In fact, chances are you still feel the impact of these people!

Our families act as a shaping force on us, just like erosion formed the Grand Canyon. They may erode our rougher edges as we move through life, or they may be part of what contributes to our rough edges! The family you grew up in was your first classroom to learn about life. You learned about values, rules, relationships, family hierarchies, ways of communication, and so much more.

Some of the lessons you taught to you were explicit, which means they were discussed openly. If you grew up in a family where the parent was judge, jury, and executioner, chances are you learned that authority meant "do this or else." It was pretty clear and openly expressed that is how things were going to be. You knew the expectations and what would happen because they were out in the open.

Other lessons are less explicit, and you had to pick them up by filling in the gaps or learning through observation and trial-and-error. These are called implicit rules. They are the ones you know not to break, even though it's never talked about. You probably know about them because of what happened when they were broken. The more implicit rules there are with less explicit, the more uncertainty and stress will be present.

Knowing about explicit and implicit rules will allow you to look at what you are doing as a father and identify your family's openness level. The clearer you are in your expectations, the less you take the guessing game out of the equation for your children. Be smart about what your explicit rules are and make sure they are ones that benefit the family. Let's explore some topics where explicit or implicit ideas may come into play without you realizing it.

### The Gender Impact

Reflect on your family of origin and look at it in a way that singles out gender. Were specific tasks broken down by gender? Were there things that anyone could take care of whereas others only boys or girls could do? What types of things were you expected to do because you were a boy that you hated doing? I know that garbage duty and cleaning up after the dogs are not my favorite, yet it always fell on the boys to get it done.

As a young boy, what was expected of you? Were you supposed to be strong athletic, and good at math and science? Was it okay if you were not interested in sports and instead wanted to do art or writing? Were you allowed to express emotions and even cry if needed? What about these questions for the girls?

Okay, so you might have noticed some strong gender stereotypes in those questions. The question is, how attached are you to some of these ideas? What is different about your thoughts on gender today? Has your behavior changed with your changes in thoughts? Your behavior will show your real thoughts; let me tell a quick story to show what I mean.

In one of my classes, one father mentioned he grew up in a home where the boys weren't allowed to show any emotion that might be seen as weak. If he had a tear in his eye, his father would smack him around, saying, "I'll give you something to cry about." He grew up believing that these types of emotions were a sign of weakness.

This dad signed up for the class because his wife had just had twin baby girls. He hoped that he could learn to be a different dad than his father was to him. During the lesson on emotions, he did not hesitate to share his childhood experiences and how his mind has changed since then. He expressed that men having feelings was okay and that it was acceptable to share them with others.

Later that night, a different participant began to cry when telling a story from his childhood. In response to these tears, this man laughed and said out loud, "come on, man, no need to cry about it." I did not have to say a word, as the other dads jumped in and mentioned how he had just said his views had changed, and yet he was acting like his father.

If you want to see if you have genuinely changed, check your behavior. Other people will know you have made the change internally when your behavior shows it externally. As you start making changes, you can use your behavior as an assessment tool to see how things are going. Ask others what they see in your behavior and if it is showing anything different. Otherwise, you will get called out just like this dad did when his words and actions didn't match up!

### The Role of a Parent

No matter the influence your father had on you, your mind started to create different blueprints. One of these blueprints was to outline what parents do when raising children. It does not always matter your background because knowing what is on your blueprint and its influence on you as a dad today is what matters.

As dads, one thing we need to consider is what we believe the role of mom is. Do you think that moms are there to nurture the children and care for the home? Where does she stand in the power hierarchy of the family? Is she higher than you, lower, or are you two the same? How does she know where you believe she stands? How do you treat her? How much of a priority are her academic, professional, and personal pursuits? The way you see mom will impact how you see yourself as a father.

Now, let's turn the focus back on you and your role as a dad. What did your childhood teach you about the role of a dad? What are your expectations, and what do you contribute to the home? Where do you fall on the power hierarchy? How does nurturing and caring for the home come into play with you? What do you provide for the family, and how do you do it? How aligned is your behavior with your views?

As you think about your ideas on moms and dads' roles, how much influence did your family growing up have on these thoughts? What have you put together about the purpose of parents? Are you there to guide and teach or control and punish? What is your purpose as a dad? How different is this from the example your father gave you? What model has other parents you have seen been in your life? Did they create any changes to your blueprint?

Your family of origin will influence the type of father you are; however, it is not destiny or set in stone. You do not have to do things the exact same way your parents did. If you want to follow in their footsteps, take action to do so. If you don't like the footsteps your parents left for you, leave better ones for your children. As you make your fathering playbook, keep what you want, get rid of what you don't, and try new things. The relationship you have with each of your children will be unique, and your playbook needs to reflect that!

The more you understand how your past influences who you are now, the more control you gain over the type of dad you are now. If you haven't already, start to map out the kind of dad you want to be. What types of stories do you hope your children tell about you? What answers do you want them to have when they're asked what it was like growing up with their dad? What do you need to do more or less of to get there?

## Why Figure This Out?

Just out of curiosity, do you know how much of an impact you can have on your child's life? Many dads I have worked with recognize they are important, but they don't always know what that entails. We are not background actors in our children's lives, and we have a powerful influence on their lives. Want to see the different ways you can change your child's life? I thought you might!

Research on positive father-involvement outcomes has exploded in the last fifteen years, leading to some incredible discoveries. I want to share some of that with you so you can see just how important you are! Your influence will start right from the beginning and give your children the advantage because infants that have a dad present in their lives have a significantly lower mortality rate. As your child grows, they are more likely to hit developmental milestones on time, especially with language and mobility. Infants and toddlers with an involved father also show higher trust and security levels, impacting their future relationships significantly!

With your positive and active involvement in your children's lives, they are significantly less likely to experience abuse or neglect than those without a positive father-figure. Being involved also means your child is less likely to have mental health concerns such as anxiety and depression, especially as you teach them how to manage stress and solve problems. You also help prevent mental health struggles because you will b actively creating increased levels of self-esteem, self-worth, and confidence in your child about their abilities and who they are.

Academically, children with an involved father have an advantage as well. Your influence will decrease your children's chances of repeating a grade while increasing their chances of graduating from high school and moving forward with college or other professional training. Other research indicates that when dads read to their children just ten minutes a day, their children will rapidly advance reading skills.

A valuable concept that the research has identified for dads is how much of a protective factor dads can be. When a positive dad is involved, children engage in risky behaviors such as drug use, underage drinking, early sexuality, and criminal behavior at dramatically lower rates than their peers without a father. Adolescent girls are also substantially less likely to have a teenage pregnancy as well!

As you start putting together in more depth how you see yourself as a father, keep in mind these incredible outcomes that your influence provides. As an Empowered Father, you need to be mindful of and actively take steps to promote these outcomes. You are helping your children grow and prepare for their future. You are laying the foundations for the blueprints they will form about life, just as you did from your family. You can change their world!

One of the benefits of knowing these things ahead of time is defining who you are and the type of father you want to be. With that in mind, it is time for you to challenge yourself a bit. Take out some paper or open a word processor because it's time to start a definition of what being a father means to you. If you have a partner, include them in the process to have even more benefits for your family!

Start to form the picture of what you being an Empowered Father looks like to you. What traits, characteristics, and roles do you have? What goals and hopes do you want to reach as a dad? How do you want relationships with your children to look now and when they are older? What are your limitations, and what are your strengths?

As you formulate your responses, think about what you are already doing well and where some change is needed. See this exercise as a work-in-progress. As you move throughout the book, add anything that stands out or what you believe is vital to you being the best dad you can be. The more you know yourself at a deeper level, the more effective you will be. That is the way to be an Empowered Father!

## Final Thoughts

As you move into the next phase of this book, where we really start to highlight what an Empowered Father is and how they work, make sure you are in a place where you can be open to ideas and finding out how they could be relevant to you. If you find yourself defensive or immediately dismissing ideas, take some time to think about why this might be the case. Change can be difficult, and at times resistance keeps us safe from the discomfort of change. Only you will know what the case is for you. We live in a time where our children need us to be the best men and fathers that we can be. Be the Empowered Father that you are and continue to rise to that challenge!

# | 3 |

# The Power of the Relationship

The relationships you have with your children will be unique in the way they grow and develop over time. No matter what you do as a father, it will somehow come back and impact the relationship. Your real power as a father comes not from your position but in the relationships you have with your children. Even though these relationships are critical, there are going to be times they don't get fed. As an Empowered Father, draw on the relationship because all the love and power you need to be the best father for your children lie there.

Every interaction you have with your child, each decision you make, the way you discipline, all the words you say, anything you do will come back and impact the relationship. The decision you have to make is whether the relationship will be your ally or your enemy. The more consistent you are in your approach and behavior that is positive and supportive to your child, the more security you will build. The more unpredictable you are, the more anxiety and stress you will cause in the relationship.

All human beings seek security in their relationships, and the more you can provide that for your children, the higher chance they are to have that in their future relationships. There is more at stake than just the moment you are in with your child. You are influencing their future in ways you may not always be thinking about. Relationships come with many complex dynamics, so to help make things a little simpler, let me introduce you to the Relational Bank Account.

## The Relational Bank Account

Many fathers I have worked with have said that the Relational Bank Account is a game-changer for them. Relationships are not always easy to conceptualize, yet this simple metaphor helps give you something tangible. The basic gist is looking at the relationship you have with your child in similar terms to a regular checking account. Let's check it out!

When your bank account has a healthy balance, how do you feel about things? What relief and security do you feel when there is still money left over after all your bills, debts, and responsibilities? It's hard not to have a smile on your face knowing you can go to a movie or eat out without worrying about what you will have to go without! What changes for you when you know you are nearing the last of your funds, and there are still bills to pay? How stressed, uncertain, and insecure do you feel?

What in the world does that have to do with our relationship with our children? Why make this comparison? It all ties to the Relational Bank Account. A healthy account means you are spending more time with your child with a positive balance than in the negative. Since this account's balance is never static and always in flux, being in the positive is a good thing. The higher the balance in this account, the more security you create for your child, similar to what you feel when you can splurge and go to the movies!

You will also feel more secure in the relationship when your balance is positive. A healthy balance typically comes with feeling like you are in a flow with your child. You enjoy spending time with them and entering their world. You make sure they are a priority, and you feel confident in the decisions you are making. Just like a real checking account, it is easier to relax and enjoy the moment when there is no stress of being overdrawn.

When the balance in the relational bank account drains and moves closer to the negative, that is when you will start to see struggles. You may find yourself yelling, feeling irritated and overwhelmed, having less patience, and handing out harsh punishments. The stress of not having enough funds in the account changes your views and reactions to the situation. What creates these constant fluxes in the relationship? That is where withdrawals and deposits come into play.

Are you wondering how you make withdrawals or deposits? That is a great question! If you do not know how to put funds back into the account or what makes them leave in the first place, you are not going to manage the budget well. If you do not learn to manage it, you're going to find yourself disconnected from your children. To help you out, let's take a closer look at withdrawals and deposits.

### Withdrawals

Spoiler alert: you want to avoid withdrawals as much as possible. This can be a difficult thing to do, but it is necessary if you're going to manage your relational accounts efficiently. The primary way that withdrawals will happen is not spending quality time with your children. Your children need to spend time with you, and they will do crazy things to get your attention if this need is starving.

Has your child ever poked you, chased the dog, hit their sibling, banged on a pot or pan nonstop, cried overdramatically, or kept saying "dad, dad, dad!" over and over? While you may find it annoying, because it is, your child is sending you an emergency message. They are urgently attempting to communicate with you. Your child is sending a bid for your attention, which means they want to make a deposit into the relationship. When you do not see it this way and ignore or snap at them, which is easy to do when the balance is low, the account's balance takes a hit. The more often you do this, the higher the amount taken out gets each time.

Critical words are another way you can take from the account, and it does not always happen intentionally. Maybe you have had a long day and try to make a joke, but instead, it turns to sarcasm and the punchline has a literal punch to it for your child. You just made a withdrawal. Perhaps your child is huge into Pokémon, and you say it is the stupidest thing in the world; that balance just took a hit. If you become overly critical or harsh during times when your child feels insecure, your balance will take a hit. This happens because your children fear coming to you rather than respecting you. Be careful with the words you say and how you say them!

Disciplining your child is another withdrawal, and a tricky one at that since there are times you have to do it. Whenever you consequence, such as sending your child to timeout, raising your voice, taking something away, keeping them home from a birthday party, or limiting Netflix, you are making a withdrawal.

Think about this way: you don't like to be disciplined at work. If it happens and not in the most respectful of ways, your view of your boss and the organization can change quickly. Your morale takes a dive, and your willingness to give back disappears. It is the same way with your children when you have to hold them to a standard.

No one likes to be corrected, and it will be a withdrawal from the relationship. The critical thing to remember, though, is how you discipline determines the size of the withdrawal. Harsher discipline will take a bigger chunk out of the relationship than positive and loving discipline. To help balance out the effects of withdrawals, you need to ensure deposits are as essential to your relationship as breathing is to life.

### Deposits

It's tempting to get stuck on how easy it is to make withdrawals, but the antidote is a lot more fun and meaningful to the relationship. You want to prevent withdrawals, and the best way to do that is to get proactive and make deposits. The great news is there are a ton of deposits you can make that are easy to do. Deposits based on togetherness and love create strong and lasting bonds between you and your child.

The best way to make a deposit is by spending quality time with your child. This makes sense, considering it is the opposite of the most common withdrawal of not being present. Quality time is not sitting on a couch on your phone while your child plays next to you. It means getting your hands dirty and entering your child's world, which is quite honestly a lot more exciting than the adult world!

To make the time you spend with your child more meaningful to them, find what your child loves, and do it with them. Play trucks, dress up during a tea party, go ride bikes, throw a football, play volleyball, have sword fights with foam noodles, work on a car together, write a play, the adventures are endless. Learn from your child what they love to do, and then join them!

Often, we think if we have them do what we want to do, we're making a considerable deposit. Chances are you are right, a deposit is being made, but it will not be as big as the one that will happen if you take a genuine interest in your child and spend time joining them in their passion. It is incredibly validating for your child when you embrace and encourage who they are as an individual.

Want to make the quality time you spend with your child, or any moment you get with them, even more meaningful? All you need to do is show affection to your child when you are with them. As crazy as it might sound, something as simple as a hug, fist bump, an arm around the shoulder, or a kiss can greatly impact the relational bank account.

For some children, physical affection is a way to create security for them because it reassures them that you love them. If your child does not start talking to you openly until you have put an arm around them or hugged them, that is a good sign that affection is a critical deposit for them. Physical affection is also powerful during the tough times when you are having a rough conversation or disciplining. I know for some of the dads I have worked with, physical affection is not the easiest thing to do, but if it is valuable to your child, it is worth giving it a shot!

When it comes to the media, dads seem to be stereotypically portrayed as comical relief who only wants to have fun. The thing is, fun is a powerful part of a strong relationship with your child. When you and your child laugh uncontrollably together or wrestle on the floor, these are rich deposits in the account. While being a dad is a lot more than just fun, don't neglect that part! Build forts out of cushions, throw snowballs at your children, play sports, have random dance parties, bring the fun in for both you and your children; you won't regret it!

There are a ton of different ways to make deposits into the relationship. It's easy to get stuck on the withdrawals and not see how easy it is to make deposits. Be there with your child, listen when they have a struggle, hold them when they get hurt, help them with their homework, listen to their stories, leave a note in their lunch, send them a random selfie, let them know you are thinking about them, greet them with a warm hug, the list is endless!

Just know this relationship always needs to be fed. If you focus too much on discipline and enforcing limits without including warmth and connection, the balance will drain quickly, and you will become more disconnected from your child. You must be diligent in putting the effort in to keep making deposits to build a strong relationship. Life with a green balance is a lot more fun than when it is in the red; let's find out why.

### Life with a Red Balance

What does it mean to have a red balance in the relational bank account? Will it be the end of your world? Not at all, but I can say it may feel like it at times because chances are, you're going to be stressed, and parenting will be a lot more strenuous. Your interactions will feel more tense and less enjoyable, which only pushes your farther into the red.

When your balance is in the red, you will notice several things. One thing you might notice is a change in the way you interact with your child. You might try to exert more authority, most likely in reaction to your child acting up more because of the red balance. Basically, if it seems like you are disciplining all the time, your balance is in the red.

When your child's acting up gets to you, and you react, you will most likely miss the real message behind their behavior. Since the balance is in the red, your child is trying to get your attention to make a deposit. Is it the most effective way? Of course not, but when it's in the red, neither of you are going to be that effective.

Another thing you might notice with life in the red is

a lack of overall fun for you and your child. Let's not kid ourselves; being a father is hard work! It is an endurance challenge that doesn't always come with gratitude or appreciation. However, there are also times it is just plain fun! When the fun levels start to decline, use this as a sign to check on your relationship's balance and start making deposits to get out of the red.

One thing to keep in mind is that there are many responsibilities on your shoulders to help manage the relationship. This is especially true if your child is younger. Your children will feel when the balance is draining and will express their insecurity around this through their behavior. When they are older, and you have taught them about the relational bank account, they may ask you to make a deposit. Overall, it will be up to you to teach your child how to build a strong and enduring relationship.

Take a few moments to reflect on the unique relationship you have with each of your children. What does it feel like when the balance is in the red? What are you doing that helps or hinders the total balance? The key is for you to get to know your relational bank accounts' patterns with each child. Learn the warning signs of when you are moving towards the red. Just as it's hard to pay a bill with an overdrawn bank account, it is hard to do what you need to as a dad with a red balance!

### Life in the Green

Have you noticed life is better when you have a positive balance in your checking account? It's nice when there isn't as much stress around getting bills paid, food on the table, and having a little leftover for some fun. The same is true for your relational bank accounts, which is why you want to spend as much time in the green as possible! Life with a green balance has a positive flow and things feel good. Even when a withdrawal is made, its impacts are not as damaging, and there is still a positive vibe to your relationship.

The way you interact with your child is a lot different when you have a green balance. Your actions and words are going to be more positive, even when you are disciplining. Unlike a red balance that usually leads us to be overly critical, we tend to be more encouraging and show affection when green. There is more fun in your relationship, communication comes easier, and both you and your child will feel secure together. Making deposits regularly means meeting each other's needs regularly, and that is when relationships feel the best!

A green balance even helps with the discipline process. Just know that a green balance does not mean there is no need to discipline. The thing that changes is your approach. Your words and consequences tend to not be as severe, and you will give some benefit of the doubt to your child, which is in contrast to life in the red, where you are more likely to be too intense. You will think differently about your child's misbehavior, focusing on what they might actually be doing versus your negative assumptions running the show like they would with a red balance.

Since the stress levels do not seem overwhelming, you are likely to have a little bit of mercy rather than only a justice perspective. You will try to see the situation more objectively and try to understand your child. That does not mean you will let them get away with murder; instead, it is more likely you will act in a way that helps the situation rather than makes it worse. Discipline can lead to a deeper connection when done in a supportive and mentoring way. Let's face it; life is better in the green!

### A Word of Caution

The relational bank account must be continuously fed. It can't get too high into the green. However, you still need to be cautious. Just as mistakes can be made with managing finances and overspending, it can happen with your relational bank accounts as well. Several things can happen when the account is feeling full and things are going well. You can become complacent, which means going on auto-pilot rather than actively engaging with your child. This replaces quality time that is focused and meaningful with lackadaisical behavior on your part. That's a withdrawal, and the balance begins to drain.

In addition to complacency, keep an eye out for spending too much time in the fun zone. While the fun zone is more entertaining, staying here will keep you from keeping your structure in place. You might be tempted to overlook when your child needs redirection. It is easy to get stuck on the balance, which keeps you from making those necessary withdrawals of discipline.

If this continues, it will torpedo your relationship and the balance will plummet. Discipline is a necessary part of fathering, do not let the fun disguise that. A high balance does not mean discipline is no longer required. You need to continue to hold the structure in place that helped foster the relationship you have with your children. If this seems unclear, don't worry, there will be more on balancing fatherhood and fun in a later chapter!

It's time to reflect on the relationships you have with your children. What are you doing differently when the balance is in the green rather than the red? How do you see your children's behavior differently? What would you like to do more of to keep building a strong balance? What struggles have you had with complacency or balancing authority and fun? What things can you do to ensure you continually feed the relationship with powerful deposits? After you've thought about those things, let's move into the role of patience in relationships.

## Patience and Relationships

We live in a world that has moved faster than it ever has before. From just the palm of your hand, you can look up any piece of information, watch tons of videos, order things you want, get food, message hundreds of people, scroll your social media feeds, download an app for anything, all within moments. Yet, even as the world has sped up, fathering has not. There can be a struggle going from a world of instant gratification to fatherhood, where you do not always get the benefits of your hard work right away. That is where patience comes into play.

Building a strong relationship takes patience. It is one of

the most challenging parts of being a father. It comes into play when you discipline, interact with your child, listen to them, and the approach you will take to reach your goals as a father. Today, dads face a strained relationship with patience as we navigate our sped-up world and the need to delay our gratification. You have to overcome instant gratification.

Without patience, fatherhood becomes even trickier. There are going to be problems you want to solve right away that can't be. Your children will test you and push you to your limits at times, and in ways you have never been pushed before. In a world where the timeframe for patience is shrinking, fatherhood will show you just how much it is still needed.

Patience impacts the long-term relationship you will have with your children. You want your children to trust you and feel like they can come to you with their toughest problems, right? I would guess you also want them to know you love them and will always have their back. To create that type of relationship, you must put a lot into the relationship now in order for it to pay off at a later time. You will be enduring times where you give more than you receive back. That is contrary to many things in the world and can be tough to manage for some.

It is normal to give more than you receive in the father-child relationship, especially when your child is younger. Just know, the more you give without seeing an immediate return, the more you might feel discouraged, stressed, or frustrated. This creates resistance to patience, especially when we want something now. Don't run from patience; let it help you embrace the long-term perspective.

If you father only for the moment, you will miss out on building the relationship you truly want. Fathering in the moment and for the future creates a powerful and lasting connection. You must father now for the relationship you want with your child in the future. If you have younger children and want a strong relationship during the teenage years, the foundations for that to happen are being laid now. Don't get lost in focusing only on the moment. Widen your focus and keep in mind the patterns you are creating today that will guide the future.

Being an Empowered Father requires you to use patience regularly. It's a powerful tool that helps you and your child. Patience helps you when you will be giving more to the relationship than you will get back. It pushes you through the frustration and when it feels like you are taking more steps backward than forwards. Be patient with yourself, your child, and with the journey of becoming an Empowered Father. You may be putting in a lot at the beginning, but the payoff will be more than worth it!

## When Do I Start Building the Relationship?

This is a question I often hear from the dads I work with, and luckily the answer is simple and requires only one word: immediately. If the only thing you do after reading this chapter, or even this book, is to build up the balance in your relational bank account, you are on the right path! Begin investing in your relationship now. I'd like to tell you a personal story about how important it is to start building the relation-ship immediately.

My wife was pregnant with our first child when this story happened. Does that seem strange? The truth is, we can start building a relationship before we even hold or see our child, so if you are a soon-to-be dad, start building it now. Back to the story! My wife and I had set a goal to have me talk to her stomach a few minutes each night before we went to bed. I won't lie; it was awkward at first, talking a stomach without any real response from the other side.

As the pregnancy progressed, I grew more comfortable with it, and as our son grew, I started seeing kicks and move-ments in response to my voice. That is an awesome experi-ence! He started moving at certain times, like when I would read or sing to him. It was a powerful feeling and created a connection, one that I would not know how important it was until the day of his birth.

When we were at the hospital to have him, things did not go to plan. Anxiety, stress, fear, exhaustion, and a lot of chaos began to replace our initial excitement as my wife went through over 30 hours of unproductive labor. He started to show signs of distress, and we made the call to have an emer-gency C-section.

We found out that he did not descend during the pro-cedure because the umbilical cord was wrapped around his neck. That was not a fun thing to learn when having a baby! Luckily, the procedure went well, and our boy was born. Since it was an emergency, neither my wife nor I got to hold him as he was rushed to the NICU right away. In the moments following this, I learned about the power of building the relational bank account.

Before I even walked into the NICU, I could head my son screaming his lungs out. Obviously, he was not happy, probably wondering what in the world was going on, and felt insecure in this strange, new world. The nurse tried hard to calm him down, but to no avail as my son was not having it. Quickly I moved close to him and stuck out my finger, which he promptly grabbed, and I will never forget the feel of that. I leaned down and calmly said, "Hey bud, it's me, your dad."

The nurse's mouth dropped open as my son immediately stopped crying, opened his eyes, and tried to look in my direction. He was still making sobbing noises, but his breathing calmed and his fingers tightened around mine even more. Just six simple words brought immediate security, comfort, and hope to my son. Why? He had never seen me before. However, he knew my voice, and he knew it was his dad. As soon as he heard me speak, he knew everything was okay.

Without building the relational bank account with him immediately, even in pregnancy, he and I would not have had that incredibly powerful moment. You must continue to build your relational bank accounts with your children, investing often for the short and long-term. There is no better time to start than now. No matter where you and your child's connection levels are now, start building that balance up immediately. The relationship is your true source of power as a dad; use it to benefit you and your child. Time to start building!

## Final Thoughts

It may seem like I have put myself on repeat here, but the relationship you have with each of your children is the foundation for all you will do as a father. Everything you do will connect and impact this relationship. It also has a dramatic impact on your children and the relationships they will have growing up, which makes sense if you look at it through the metaphor of the relational bank account.

If a child has gone through life with their accounts full and deposits were regularly made, they will know what it takes to keep their future relational accounts with others full, including their children. However, if a child grows up with an account in the red, they become overly familiar with it. They get used to insecurity and disconnect, and their future relationships may show this pattern as well. Without a lot of experience in the green or making deposits, they will draw on what they know, making withdrawals. Your relationship with your child has a lot of power; yield it responsibly!

The ideas and concepts covered in this book's remaining chapters need to be read and viewed through a relationship lens. Everything you do will impact it, and the hope is to take the ideas and tools to create powerful bonds with your children. There will be ideas you agree with more than others; all I ask is that you take the time to consider ideas and then find ways to use the ones you think would help you and your child the most.

Before moving forward into the next chapter, take some time now to think about your relational bank accounts with your children. How are you adding or taking away from them? What insights and take-aways you have had from this chapter that you can put into action now? The longer you wait to act, the less likely it will happen. Failing to act prevents you from having the relationships with your children that you want.

Keep investing and adding deposits to the relationship. The more you do this, the faster you will see why Empowered Fathers turn to the relationship before anything else. Remember, anything you do will impact the relationship you have with your children. It is not about you as a dad or your child's behavior. It's about the relationship. Get out there, start investing, and build the relationships that will change your children's lives!

# | 4 |

# Values, Morals, Beliefs, and Goals

Who do you want to be as a dad? What defines you? Two simple questions that have a ton of depth to them the more you think about them. This chapter will take you on an inner journey to help you find out who you are, what you stand for, and what you want as a man and as a father.

As each of us travels through life, we have internal guides that help us make decisions. These guides help us choose friends and partners, identify career paths, what you should do in challenging situations, and any other choice life likes to throw our way. The more connected you are to these internal guides, the easier it will be to use them in meaningful ways. The less connected you are, the more lost and confused you might feel in your life. These guides are your values, morals, beliefs, and goals.

Often we know we have these guides in our life, but the question is, have we taken the time to think them through and connect with them? Usually, the answer is no, and we run on auto-pilot with these unknown guides running in the background. Sometimes there is nothing wrong with this, and other times they go off like a landmine. Have you ever reacted strongly to your child and didn't know why? That is what happens when there was a violation of a core part of you, even if you were not aware of it because it is in the background.

This chapter is meant to help you identify the guides you always have going and connect with them so they are not just running unknown and freely in the background. These guides are always at work, and as an Empowered Father, it would benefit you to be aware and connect with them.

You might even find the need to challenge some of your guides because they do not always develop in beneficial ways. This is especially true concerning the father-child relationship. I'm asking you to approach this chapter with an open mind and a willingness to explore these guides and what they are doing for you. Keep in mind that while we will talk about values, morals, beliefs, and goals separately, in reality, they work together to influence our lives. Let's do this!

## Values

Everyone has a set of values that guides their lives. Our lists of values will all be unique and will not have the same ones or ranked in the same order. Some of our values are incredibly precious to us, which is both extraordinary and troublesome as it makes it hard to see any need to adjust them when necessary. Each value on our list comes with its own meaning and significance, some of which are locked down like Fort Knox and others that are fluid and flexible.

Your values are the things in life that are important to you and bring value. They are the things you hold highly in your life and could include family closeness, work, religion, independence, privacy, trust, responsibility, respect, and the list goes on and on. Your values build a framework for how you will develop, express, and live your morals and beliefs. Where do these values come from? We get them from several sources, and we'll highlight just a few here.

You won't be surprised to find out that the family you grew up in is a primary source of your values. For example, if you grew up in a home where family comes first, chances are you are going to raise your children with that view. Based on your childhood experiences, you have selected values you like and let go of those you did not. What values would you say you have carried on from the family you grew up with?

Your social circle also influences your values. Participating in things like politics, education, religion, or philanthropy shapes the values you see or express. The reinforcement you get from these different circles can help you internalize your values more or find new ones.

Life comes with a lot of experiences. As you have moved throughout your life, you have tried out new things to find out who you are. This includes trying out different values and seeing how they fit or how others received them. Some of the reactions you got were positive, and others probably not as much. Your different experiences helped shape who you are and what values you hold. Just know your children are going to go through the same process when it comes to their values!

Here's a simple yet effective exercise to get to know your values system as a father. Take time to reflect on some of the values you hold, and then list them out. Once you have them listed, go through the following questions and write down any thoughts you want to remember. Getting to know who you are helps you understand what you'll do in different situations!

When you look at your values, can you identify if they came from your family, social circles, experience, or another source? How has your experience helped shape the values you currently hold? What values on your list could benefit from being challenged or modified? How aligned is your behavior with your values? How are you living your values as a father? Keep this exercise around; you're going to use it again a little later in this chapter!

## Morals

Your morals are your guide for what you believe to be right or wrong and good or bad. When you were a young child, chances are your morals were black and white. However, as you grew up and experienced life, your morals will have grown more complicated, and you most likely see a lot of gray areas rather than just black and white.

Your children are starting to adopt their morals, and the younger they are, the less gray area they will see. This can cause some tension amongst you and your children, as both your views tend to contrast. To help ease this type of stress and help you know how you will approach the situation, you need to connect with your own set of morals.

It seems that morals typically come with a "do not" in front of them. Do not lie, do not steal, do not cheat, or do not harm others. These morals provide the road signs for your internal guides as you navigate life. As you grew up, your morals, just like your values, have been influenced by different parts of your life. The family you grew up with is where the foundations of your morals were laid.

Interestingly enough, we can learn about morals from the opposite behaviors people close to us show. I worked with a child in therapy who let me know that "we do not steal, it's very bad," a moral that was adopted due to their parent being incarcerated for theft.

We start to teach our children about morals early on and reinforce them throughout their life. If we become overly rigid with our morals, we need to be aware that this could cripple our children in having the flexibility they need to navigate the world outside of our walls. Life today with a lot of different distractions, many of which are presented early to children. Sex, drugs, alcohol, violent behavior, poor attitudes towards school or authority, pornography, bullying, and so many other trials await our children once they are out of our door. Being too rigid in enforcing our morals can hinder the growth process needed to help children navigate the different challenges they will face and potentially push them in another direction as they seek to rebel against you!

While being too rigid may lead children to want to bend the boundaries, that does not mean we cannot be firm. While it may sound the same, having firm morals means we stand our ground while also understanding that the world does not work in black and white. It leaves room for our children to figure their lives out. We need to be clear in understanding our morals and how our experiences have shaped them so that we can help our children form theirs.

Our morals change with time as we learn and grow. Perhaps we adopt a new moral that is more in-line with who we are as a person. Maybe we grew up without a lot of morals and have since adapted more, or perhaps the opposite is true. Having an understanding of this helps us as we watch our children grow. They are going through the same process as we are, and we can help guide them rather than impress what we want on them.

Take out the values exercise you worked on earlier. It's time to reflect on your moral development. Where do you believe your morals have come from? Who has helped influence them the most? How have they changed throughout your life? Would you consider yourself rigid, flexible, or permissive in your morals? How will this come into play for you as a father?

## Beliefs

Our beliefs are the ideas we have on how things should or should not be. We have views related to ourselves, others, and how relationships work. A lot of our behavior is based on our beliefs, and the less clarity we have, the more we are prone to *react* rather than look at a situation objectively. We need to become familiar with our beliefs to be a better man and father for our children.

The Empowered Father can look at his beliefs and modify or delete those that need it while simultaneously integrating those that are beneficial and working. This is not done once in life and then you are good to go from then on. This needs to become an on-going process throughout your life. If we neglect to look at our beliefs, our child moving through different life stages will call on it for us. The main difference is if we wait for our child's development to jumpstart us, we are more likely to be unprepared than if we make it part of our lives.

Whenever our child meets a new life stage like talking, school, puberty, adolescence, or leaving home for the first time, we will be forced to look at our own beliefs. As an Empowered Father, take a proactive approach and begin to look before these different development periods come to prevent *reacting.* When we *react,* we are less effective as fathers and problem-solvers and more effective at damaging the relationship. Instead, by being proactive, we are more effective as fathers and problem-solvers and less effective at damaging the relationship, exactly what we want!

Let's take a quick look at some important beliefs we need to assess. There will be overlap with these beliefs, which is okay because these are not all you will be facing as a dad. Just keep in mind as we explore them that they are not happening independently of one another. Like all the other constructs in this book, there is an interaction that creates the picture of who we are and what we will do!

### Beliefs about Being a Man

Let's start by talking about being a man. This is a topic that has become a political hot button, and this is all the more reason you need to lock it down. What does it mean to you to be a man? What traits and characteristics are part of being a man? What're your responsibilities as a man?

Forming this idea of what it means to us regarding being a man provides a window into our priorities and where we want to head in life. Take the simple example of the belief that a man should be successful. What does this mean to you? Is a successful man one who puts their family first and has a promising career, or can achieve personal and professional goals? How would your view on this impact you as a father?

One reason why we must get to know what it means to us to be a man is to understand how this influences our children. The views we have will dictate how we behave, which communicates to our children messages regarding masculinity. The more aware we are of our beliefs, the more intentional we can be about the messages we want to send. It is our responsibility to teach them about what it means to be a man for those of us with sons. They will begin to piece together their thoughts and views on the matter by watching the man that means the most to them: you. The way you behave, treat others around you, talk about manhood, and carry yourself will help form these early beliefs. This is an enormous responsibility that the Empowered Father understands is his when he has a son. We must help show the path for the next generation of what it means to be a man.

There is also an essential responsibility for those with daughters. Not only will we help them formulate what masculinity in the world means, but we also demonstrate to them what is acceptable or expected when it comes to being treated by a man. Our daughters' relationship is a valuable foundation for teaching our young women how other males in their life should treat them. As Empowered Fathers, we strive to provide a respectful and healthy portrayal of masculinity by giving an example of love and openness. Understanding our views of what it means to be a man impacts more than just who we are. It has a substantial effect on how our children will grow to see the world and navigate their journey of figuring out who they are. Figuring out what it means to be a man is just the start; we need to know how this translates into what it means to be a father.

### *What it means to be a Father*

This is a chance for you to revisit the definition you started for yourself as an Empowered Father. Your definition will give you a preview of the beliefs you have about fatherhood. You can add to this definition with the following questions. What are some of your beliefs about fatherhood? What does a father do? How do we teach our children? These are the types of questions that do not have one right answer. It is up to you to connect with your responses about your beliefs and find out how they are part of you. The more aligned you are with your values, morals, and beliefs, the more effective you will be as an Empowered Father!

Let's take a look at one of the most common beliefs about

being a father I have heard when working with dads. This belief centers on the need to be a coach and a teacher to our children. Was that on your list? This gives us the responsibility to act as a coach and mentor as we help guide our children through life to help them learn how to conquer the struggles and obstacles that come their way to prepare them for adulthood. What does this mean to you? Where does it fit in with your beliefs? Let's take this discussion about fatherhood even deeper by looking at a complicated topic: power.

### Fatherhood and Power

Power is a unique word when it comes to fatherhood. It is a slippery concept that can be held firmly in one moment and lost entirely in the blink of an eye. The power we have allows us to connect with our children, hold them accountable to expectations, and use discipline when necessary. It is easy to draw on power that is based on authority and use it in an attempt to force our children to do what we want them to do. For this reason, we must ask ourselves the following questions. What are my views and beliefs about the relationship between power and being a father? The Empowered Father sees the relationship as the real source of power; what does this mean to me?

The more we draw on positional power, the more rigid we are likely to be. The following are several examples of more rigid beliefs about fatherhood and power observed in my work with fathers. The key is to look for words that signify rigidity rather than flexibility, such as always or never. After reading these examples, take an honest look at your beliefs and behaviors to see if there is any rigidity. If you find yourself defensive, that might be a clue for you!

*"Since I am the father, my child should never disobey me."*

*"My way or the highway."*

*"My child should always do what I ask of them or be prepared for the consequences."*

*"With enough whoopings, my child will learn to respect me and learn it good."*

*"My children will always listen to me; I am the boss."*

Some of these beliefs may seem exaggerated, but it is crucial to assess your views' similarities. It is not uncommon to start with beliefs that do not appear as intense as these only to have them grow more rigid as our children develop. These rigid beliefs will most likely show their face when arguing with your child. When we feel disrespected, caught off guard, let down, or disappointed, we may draw on a belief such as "my child should always do what is asked of them; I am the father!" Unfortunately, this is where a paradox comes into play. The paradox is that the more rigid we get, the more likely we will get more of what we do not want from our child. This means we double down on control and the cycle goes on and on!

Take another look at those examples of power beliefs. What type of power are these beliefs drawing from? Will the power being used benefit the relationship between father and child or take away from it? When a father uses power based on rank, threats, intimidation, and potentially physical means, the questions that need to be asked are how effective this method is and why we do it?

When we look at power and being a father, we need to look at the relationship we have with our child. If we power from only authority to get our point across, we are making bigger withdrawals from our relational bank account than necessary. Remember what happens when our relational bank accounts get overdrawn and our relationship breaks down? Our children are less likely to feel our love and connected to us, leading to even less compliance and following the rules. This may lead to more power methods as we *react* with frustration and anger rather than taking a step back. It will take a lot of repair work in the future to try and undo what we could have prevented in the beginning.

A positive, healthy relationship with our child provides the source of power necessary that we need as a father. As fathers, when we balance our authority with the connection that benefits the relational bank account, we can draw on a different power type. This type of power is based on respect, integrity, and love, empowering our children and ourselves.

As you can see, our beliefs about power have dramatic impacts on how we will father. An Empowered Father understands their views, where some changes need to be made and makes those changes. To do this, we need to look at our willingness to be flexible and make life changes.

### Beliefs about Being Flexible

This belief is not about gymnastics! A healthy level of flexibility means we are open to changing some of our views to grow as a man and a father. However, if we are too flexible, we may not know where we actually stand and depend on people on the outside to help direct us. This can be just as risky because we do not learn more about who we are personally and become a creation of what is around us. We must find a healthy balance of being open to new ideas without sacrificing the man and the father we are at our core, a tough thing to do!

Without flexibility, we move into rigid territory. At this point, we are no longer open to hearing or learning about different ideas and views. There is no room for growth since we believe that we are already where we want to be and change is unnecessary. The process of becoming an Empowered Father cannot happen when we are too rigid. There must be continual growth, and it will be a process that continues for our entire life. If our views are rigid and we think we have already arrived at our destination, we will miss what more there is to learn. Being rigid does not allow for growth or learning, which is necessary as our children grow and develop. Instead, see resistance as a chance to challenge yourself and see what alternatives there are. Let's face it; rigidity will only hinder us when it comes to fathering children!

### Beliefs about Children and their Behavior

One thing that influences the views we have about our children and our expectations of them is what we think we know about children in general. Whether aware of them or not, you have guiding beliefs about how children should act based on their age. However, a lot is going on throughout your child's development. If you are unfamiliar with child development and the physical, emotional, psychological, and social milestones at given stages, it would be prudent to re-search this information. As this topic is beyond this book's scope, you can do a quick internet search that will provide you with information on child development.

The more we know about child development, the more realistic our expectations will be. As fathers, we often look at our children's behavior through our adult lens. For example, we know it is cold outside when there is snow on the ground, which means it would be smart to wear a coat. Our children are still learning, which means a three-year-old does not get this as intuitively as you do. We need to acknowledge and un-derstand that our children are not miniature adults; they are children. They are learning to navigate the world, just as you did at one point. Your adult brain was formed through lots of experience that they are just starting to have!

It is easy for us to think that children are simply small adults and should know how to act appropriately. For ado-lescents, we may believe that they are smarter and know bet-ter than to try out some of their behaviors. The fact is a lot of our children's misbehavior is not out of manipulation, de-viance, or some other negative belief. For many children, it is them navigating their developmental stage, seeking out au-tonomy, learning the ropes of the world, or seeking to have a need met.

Empowered Fathers seek to learn about child develop-ment to know what is realistic for their children. This allows us to be appropriate in our expectations and recognize warn-ing signs for development concerns that professionals may need to address. Take the time to research child development and make adjustments as necessary in your fathering. If we have had unrealistic expectations or made some mistakes, it's time to make a repair.

### Father's and Apologizing

Apologizing to another person means we are genuinely stating our sorrow and regret for what we have done to them. We are taking accountability for the harm we have done to the other person. A genuine apology is hard to do since it requires us to swallow our pride and set aside our ego for a moment to admit that we were wrong in some way. Something that, let's face it, us men find hard to do.

As fathers, we will face the decision to apologize or not more than once in our lifetime. There are times we will overreact and let our anger get the best of us, forget to do something with our child, or fail to follow through on a promise. We need to know ahead of time whether or not we believe that it is vital for us to apologize to our children.

There have been many fathers I have worked with that do not believe we must apologize when we have done something wrong. There seems to be the belief that as the father, we are entitled to certain exemptions. A contrasting thought to consider is what our children learning if we do not apologize. When they see us do something wrong and we do not make some form of amends for that, our children will begin to internalize the belief that they do not need to either. There are short-term and long-term consequences of this.

In the short-term, our children will not apologize when they do something like yell or throw a toy at us. Even if we get upset and demand an apology, they will not see the need to apologize based on what they have seen us do with others. The act of apologizing requires us to take accountability for our actions. When we teach our children that apologies are not necessary, we deprive them of the lesson of accountability.

If we continue with this pattern long-term, our children will not see the need to apologize in future relationships either. They will demand respect and apologies just like we have shown them but will not necessarily give them in return. They seek to place blame on others rather than to see what they can do about their wrongdoings. A lot of this is preventable by demonstrating the importance of apologizing, as long as you are genuine!

When we take the time to humble ourselves, get down on our child's level, and genuinely apologize to them for something that we have done wrong, we provide a powerful model for them. We teach them about accountability, what it means to make amends, and the power of repairing a relationship. We also make a deposit into our relational bank account when we reconnect with our child, soothe their fears or disappointments, and demonstrate that we still care and love them. This is a powerful reassurance at a time when they might feel insecure.

There is a lot of benefit to apologizing, as long it is genuine. When we do not give sincere apologies, there is no repair to the relationship. Our children will know we are not being real and will instead be more likely to believe that how we initially acted is more in line with how we truly feel.

Don't be a "but-head" father when apologizing to your children. When we throw in the word "but," we undo the thought that came before it. This will more than likely undo the repair attempt that we went for in the first place. Take a look at the difference between a "but-head" apology and a genuine one.

Apology #1: *"I'm sorry son that I yelled at you, but what you did just got me so angry, and that is why I yelled."*

Apology #2: *"I'm sorry that I yelled at you, son. I let my anger get the best of me in this situation. While we will still address what has happened, I wanted to let you know that I went over the line."*

The first apology starts decently with the father letting their son know there is something they feel sorry for, and then the word "but" throws off the whole apology. It is a key-word that lets our child know that instead of apologizing, we are getting ready to justify what we did. That is precisely what happens in the final part of the apology as the father turns the responsibility of yelling over to the child. This father was only pretending to take accountability while, in reality, he was justifying his actions because of his child's behavior. That means he was also teaching his child to look for someone to blame for their behavior!

Take a moment to reread the second apology and see what you notice about the language. This father uses "I" multiple times to keep the situation of yelling on their shoulders. The first apology utilized an "I-you-I" approach: "I" did this because "you" did that, which is why "I" had to do what I did. It's false accountability. The second apology demonstrates the father keeping accountability and letting the child know it was the father who went too far with the yelling. This apology does not allow the child free from their responsibility, either.

There will still be a discussion on what will be done about the child's behavior and the situation at hand.

Using the first type of apology leads our child to be more resistant and defiant because our words have pointed the finger of blame at them, damaging the relationship. The second apology demonstrates to the child a willingness to be humble and admit when you are wrong. It keeps the integrity of your child and yourself intact. When we feel our integrity has been acknowledged and protected, we are not as resistant and defiant as when we feel blamed. There are not many better ways to be an Empowered Father and empower our children than keeping everyone's integrity intact!

Before we move onto goals, take some time to look through your beliefs. Did any of these topics surprise you or create some insight? Write that down! What do you believe is going well, and where is there room for change? If change is needed, the next section will be of help to you!

## Goals

Being goal-oriented helps us manage the various roles, responsibilities, and demands we have on our time. Goals can be broad and take time to get too, or they can be small and take only a few moments to complete. One area where it benefits us to set goals for yourself is as a father. Here are a few questions that might help you out with this. What do you want to be for our children? What do you want for yourself as a father? What's your overall vision and the steps necessary to get you there?

Now, take a moment to pause and notice that the goals these questions focus on is you. It is easy to confuse setting goals for ourselves versus for our children. It is normal and powerful to have hopes and dreams for our children; however, we must be open to the idea of letting them find the goals they have for themselves. If we prescribe their future for them through goals we set on their behalf, it will most likely lead to disappointment for both! Let me tell you a quick story about a client that illustrates this point.

A young man came into my office to work on managing his symptoms of depression and anxiety. He was a medical student and about halfway through his second semester. He had always been a 4.0 student and a high achiever, yet strangely he barely survived his first semester. Depressive symptoms began to emerge near the end of his first semester, and with the second semester not going any better, his hope and joy for life were starting to fade.

When asked what parts of medical school he enjoyed, he shook his head and replied nothing at all. As you might guess, becoming a doctor was not this young man's passion. When I asked him why he wanted to be a doctor, his response was telling. He said that it was not his passion; it was his parents. For as long as he could remember, his parents told him that he would be a doctor to continue the family legacy. His life map had already been created with a destination marked. His parents spoke of nothing less than this, leaving him one role to play for his life. He played that part well until recently, with the façade collapsing and him coming through my door.

This young man had a passion for music and teaching and saw himself working with elementary school children. When asked why he chose not to pursue this, he nearly had a panic attack in my office. He said he could not risk losing the love of his parents by deviating from their plan.

Now, think about that for a minute. This young man was so concerned about not disappointing his parents by leaving the path they had set for him that he was willing to sacrifice his hopes and dreams to satisfy them. It got to the point where he interpreted his parents' love as being available to him as long as he followed their path. Any deviation would lead to a termination of their love. Sound a bit extreme?

Okay, this may be a bit of an extreme example; however, it provides a glimpse into why we need to identify goals for us and separate them from our children's dreams. If we prescribe to our children how their life should be, we will be more likely to lead them into a life of unhappiness and struggle. This happens because we take control of their life rather than handing that control over to them. Would you want someone to dictate the path of your life without you having any say?

Taking the time to focus on the goals we have for ourselves as fathers help prevent this. Our goals should be focused on our behavior, values, reactions, or contributions to the relationship we have with each of our children. While our goals will influence our children, it will not dictate to them what they should be. Setting goals for ourselves leads us to act in ways that support our child and their goals. We support our children's hopes and are there for them when they need it.

The goals you set for yourself as a father should also have the ability to strengthen your children and the relationships you have with them. This helps you move towards being the best father you can be! Be cautious in how you construct your goals. If you set goals that are too low, you will not reach your full potential and limit your children's growth and development. Set the bar too high, and you will potentially stop because you are not perfect, and the stress and weight lead to discouragement. There are ways around this so you can REACH your goals!

### REACH Your Goals

Our goals need to stretch us, be growth opportunities, and have clarity and purpose. When we use the REACH Method of setting goals, we increase our chances of reaching not only our desired outcome but so much more! Here are the five steps to REACH your goals:

- *Recognize what goal is needed.* The first step is knowing what needs our focus. Examples may be spending time with your child, using different forms of discipline, re-arranging your priorities, or being more involved in their academics. Again, notice how these goals are focused on your behavior as the father. Recognize what goal is needed and start there.

- *Evaluate and re-evaluate.* As you work on your goal, continue to assess where you are at in your progress. Is your plan of attack working? How do you know? What changes need to be made? Do not make the mistake of evaluating options and outcomes only once. Make it a regular part of your process!

- *Adaptive planning.* This is where the principle of flexibility on our part comes into play once more. Make sure there is room in your action plan to adjust to the obstacles you will face. Life likes to throw curveballs, and you need to have the freedom and ability to change your game. Also, make the necessary changes after you evaluate and re-evaluate. This will help you accommodate new information and needs that come up.

- *Components.* Break down your goals into manageable components that will help you see and make progress. Often, we make umbrella goals, meaning our primary goal is too broad and covers too many things. This is a quick path to discouragement! Break it down into components. If your goal is spending more time with your child, break that into smaller parts. What kind of time do you want to spend with them? For example, is it more personal or homework time? Is there a certain amount of time you want to be spending with them? Are there activities or interests of theirs you want to know more about? Break it down into manageable components to keep yourself moving forward!

- *Hit the mark!* Break the goal down, evaluate, change when needed, but most importantly, put in the work to hit the mark! You will not see your plan through if there is no action. This can be one of the most challenging steps, as it is asking you to endure the struggles, but it will be the most impactful part as you feel yourself conquering what you set out to do! Our goals get us out of our comfort zones as they stretch us. Growth does not occur when we stay in place; we need to be tested and pushed beyond our comfort zone. As your children grow older, the action items of your goals will need to change. The REACH Method will help you out here as it is built to grow with you and your children. Take the time to assess where you are in your goals and what is going well and where you can improve. Develop in your mind the types of relationships you want to have with your children when they are older and start acting now in ways that will foster that! Our goals are long-term investments to bolster our relational bank accounts!

## Final Thoughts

It is essential to pull together what you value, your morals, your different beliefs, and the goals that guide your actions. The clearer you are about these topics, the more your behavior will reflect that. When your behavior is genuine and congruent with your internal views, you act in an empowered manner. You know the why to what you are doing. This won't be done overnight, and you will need to be consistent with the process. Continue to learn, grow, and challenge yourself in new ways!

# | 5 |

# How Do You Feel About Emotions?

As men, we like to speak our minds about politics, sports, weather, entertainment, and most of what crosses our minds. Emotions are not usually one of those likely topics, though. Nothing disrupts a group of guys like lobbing in a "guys, I want to talk about my feelings" grenade. The question I am proposing is, why?

Why do men not want to talk about emotions? Where does this aversion come from? Is it coded into our DNA? Of course not! What is coded in our DNA is the ability to experience a broad spectrum of emotions. Feelings of happiness, joy, boredom, sadness, anger, grief, frustration, and loss are just a small sample of the emotions you can experience.

So, if emotions are part of our experience in life, why is it that we have difficulty showing or sharing our emotions? Let's go back in time to when you were a child. As you were growing up, what were you taught about feelings and being a boy? Was there a connection between the two?

I have asked this question to hundreds of men. A small percentage have answered that they grew up in a family where emotions were openly expressed and talked about. This sounds great, except that some of these men followed that up by saying this was a problem when they moved into adolescence and none of their male friends agreed. This led to developing a struggle with emotions later in life.

Other men responded they have been able to move through life without any problems with emotions. While they are a minority in their experiences and comfort with feelings with the men I have worked with, they show us that we can experience and process emotions. There is no deficit in our DNA. However, a large majority of the men I've asked this question to have had a different experience with emotions.

Most of the men respond in a negative way towards emotions and any questions or discussions about them. Common themes about emotions in their lives are:

- Do not show them
- Emotions are for girls
- Shove them down
- Boys don't cry

Often these messages have been implicit in their lives, meaning they were not necessarily said out loud. Typically, their male role models emphasized solving problems and being analytic rather than showing emotion. Many of these men were met with sarcastic comments that alluded to the need to turn off their emotions.

Others got these same messages about emotions expressed

directly to them. These men had dads or other male role models tell them to suck it up and stop being a girl. Some were even met with physical punishment to reinforce the lesson that men do not show emotions.

What do you remember hearing about emotions as a child? As men, we are often faced with these messages early in life, and it can become a guiding belief in our lives. It also means we might be sending these messages to others around us, including our children. The good news is these messages are only as permanent as we make them. We can edit out what we do not want and put in what we do. The key is we have to want to do this and have the courage, openness, and patience it takes to challenge these old messages. To help you with this, let's look more at those messages you got as a child.

### Boys Don't Cry!

The messages we've incorporated about emotions influence the way we live and behave. Part of that comes from the way these messages teach us to cope with emotions. What does that mean? If you were told that men shove their feelings down, what do we do when we feel something? We shove it down and hide them because boys don't cry. What do you think goes through a boy's mind when he has heard these messages and has strong emotions? How does that change how he looks at himself? What if this was your son?

Following the guidance of these messages takes a toll on you over time. It may feel right at the moment to shove down unwanted emotions, and you might even think you have gotten away with it. Unfortunately, the truth is that you do not.

In physics, thermodynamics' first law states that energy cannot be created or destroyed and can only be transformed. As crazy as it sounds, emotions operate on this same principle.

To help demonstrate this, let's use loss as an example. When we experience loss, such as a loved one's death, it comes with deep sadness and grief. Following the rules of shoving emotions down, this loss leads us to take that sadness and grief and push it down. We mask it with others by saying things like we are fine, and there's no need to worry because we are okay. We hope that the discomfort of the emotions will go away after a while.

However, the power of emotions cannot be destroyed, just like energy can't because emotions are energy. Since emotions are energy that can't be destroyed, over time, they transform into something new. The sadness and despair we have shoved down are us shaking up a can of soda. The energy builds up and eventually explodes, transforming our previous emotions into anger that leaves quite a mess for ourselves and those around us.

Holding your emotions in or pretending they do not exist impacts your day-to-day functioning. Your body's chemistry changes as the energy transforms into increased stress, which causes the release of cortisol and other hormones. The converted energy of suppressed emotions creates headaches, loss or increase in appetite, stomach aches, tightness in the chest, sleeping less or more than usual, and an increase in anxious and depressing thoughts. You can destroy your physical health by suppressing and not managing your emotions.

The following story came from a dad in a class I taught and is a powerful metaphor. He had fallen on tough times and experienced several losses simultaneously in the form of a broken relationship, losing his children in a custody battle, and the death of a parent. Instead of allowing himself to experience and process the loss, he just kept telling himself and others that he was fine and handling it all. After a while, he found out that he was wrong and came up with this metaphor to describe his experience.

He said that each loss he went through was like a separate backpack he had to put on. Each day without handling emotions, he said it felt like someone was putting a two-pound rock in each bag daily. It didn't seem too bad after the first few days and gave a false illusion that you are carrying it and getting stronger. However, each bag's weight with enough time eventually becomes too much, and you crumble under the pressure and the weight of unprocessed loss. How might this metaphor be relevant to you?

Since emotion is part of the human experience, you should find a way to manage your emotions healthily and constructively. Of course, some feelings by their nature are uncomfortable and harder to handle, which increases the temptation to shove them down. Resist this temptation and do not shove them down or try to ignore them.

It would be best if you learned how to use emotions in a way that allows you to adapt and experience your life to the fullest. It helps to have a few tools in your toolbox that help you regulate and cope with your emotions. Luckily, you can do powerful things that you might find are game-changers rather than game enders. Let's check them out!

**Managing Our Emotions**

If we were to brainstorm healthy ways of expressing and coping with emotions, what ideas would you have? That's what this section is about, and we will start with the most common answer I've heard: exercise. Physical exercise is one of the best ways to reduce our body's stress from accumulated emotional baggage. There are plenty of ways to get exercise into your life, such as lifting weights, riding bikes, running, hiking, cardio, and so much more. Exercise helps us feel better about ourselves, uses up some testosterone, and keeps our minds and bodies healthy.

Men cope with hobbies, like working on cars, playing music, woodworking, cooking, writing, or countless other things. A healthy way to experience emotion is to express through an activity we are doing, such as hobbies. To get the full benefit, we need to be more present with the activity and open to what is going on within our minds and bodies. Allow yourself to experience the emotions through the journey and see what happens!

If spirituality, prayer, or meditation is valuable to you, keep doing it because these are meaningful outlets! If you have not tried some of these before, give it a go. There are thousands of years of human history demonstrating the power of meditation. A simple Google or YouTube search will connect you with different ways to meditate so you can find the right path for you.

Other ways that men express and cope with their emotions include listening to music, writing, drawing, painting, going out with friends, walking in nature, connecting with your partner, avoiding drugs and other harmful toxins, having safe and uplifting sex, and journaling. The key is to make sure that what you choose to do is done healthily to you and those around you. This brings us to an important point.

Emotions that are harder to deal with, such as sadness, loss, guilt, shame, or fear, tend to come with the temptation to isolate. Our insecurity with these feelings leads to us wanting to be an island and not let people into our world. Isolating leads us to retreat into the deepest part of ourselves and essentially become a dormant volcano. The truth is, choosing to isolate means also choosing to set ourselves up for failure. Each of us has people in our lives who care about us, and they will try to help when they notice a change in us.

Since isolation means getting stuck in our negative feelings, our frustrations are compounded when someone attempts to talk to us and ask if we are okay. This creates mounting pressure inside us until we can't take it anymore and end our isolation by erupting like a volcano. When this happens, we are left with a bigger problem than we started with. This leaves a trail of devastation with those closest to us.

Let's clear up a quick point here. There are times where it is acceptable to withdraw for some time and process what we are experiencing. Emotions are a reaction to something, and sometimes we need to work through what we are experiencing. There is a simple way to get this space in a healthy way rather than merely isolating ourselves. All you need to do is tell those closest that you need time and space alone.

As weird as it might seem, keeping a connection with others even when you need space will help provide the room you need. This will help avoid the volcano effect too! The difference between space and isolation is how you communicate with others. If you are isolating, you are breaking off contact with no communication and rarely processing your experience. Asking for space is taking the time to process what you are going through while letting others know about that need. Just remember the key with space is you have to come back and reconnect. Also, do not hesitate to contact a professional counselor if some of your experiences are too much. Helping yourself teaches your children that it is essential to ask for help when needed!

While this is by no means a complete list of ways to manage your emotions, it is an excellent place to start. There is a warning we need to keep in mind, though. Any tool that you choose can be used appropriately or inappropriately. These coping skills become inappropriate when they are a different way to mask your isolation. They also become a problem when you engage in only one or two of them far too frequently. The key to these techniques is to use them to move forward towards growth and progress.

Make sure to use multiple tools instead of relying only on one or two. The more you use the same tool over and over, the less effective it will be with time. Once your chosen tool becomes ineffective, you might fall back into your old ways and messages regarding emotions. Experiment and try out different tools to see what works for you!

Understanding, expressing, and sharing your emotions does not have to be as scary as reading a Stephen King horror novel at one in the morning on a stormy night. If you have avoided emotion in your life like it was the plague, you've got some hard work ahead of you. Just know that the journey is worth it, and you can make it through. Let's talk about how our emotions affect our children and us as dads to illustrate further why this is important.

## Emotions and Fatherhood

With some of the messages we were raised with regarding emotions, it is crucial to see how this impacts the father-child relationship. We will break this discussion down into two different topics to help make it as straightforward as possible. These two topics will be the impact emotions have on our relationship and the direct impact our emotions have on our children.

### Emotions and the Father-Child Relationship

Being the father of a child is one of the most amazing and unique relationships we can ever have in this life. In working with dads, I have found that this discussion of our emotions impacting this relationship is where they find their negative messages about emotions might be hindering them. When this happens, there is an increased motivation to edit their beliefs about emotions and make the necessary changes in their behavior. Let's see if it can do the same for you by looking at how our emotions impact our relationship through the ways we communicate, discipline, and encourage our children.

*Impacts on Communication.* Communication is the way

humans transfer different thoughts, ideas, and beliefs to one another. It happens every day, and yet it is still one of the most challenging parts of relationships. We deliver messages through our words, body language, and tone. As we communicate, there are times what we think we are conveying is not what is being received by the other. Communication is a large part of the relationships we have with our children. So, how do emotions come into play?

When we have not managed our emotions, it can have detrimental effects on the way we communicate. When we are unable to control the emotions and stressors of life, the pressure builds up. This leads to the volcano we have already described. One of the ways this volcano becomes devastating is through our communication. When we erupt, our words, body language, and tone change dramatically.

When we finally erupt, our vocabulary increases in intensity, especially when disciplining our children. We add in words and labels we would not typically say with a cooler head. We turn simple statements like "I am upset that you did not clean your room" into "I am so mad that you don't do anything that is asked of you; you're so lazy!" What do our children hear when we say something like this? How does it make them feel about themselves?

Not only do the words we say increase in intensity, so does our tone and body language. We deliver our messages in a volume that induces fear in our child. They start to fear rather than respect us and avoid the problem rather than solve them. When our words and tone intensify, our body language comes along for the ride. You might sense this by noticing your jaw tightens, fists clench, chest puffs our, or your eyes stare intensely. Our children see these changes in our body language and either rise to meet it or become submissive and hide in fear. Either way, your relational balance just took a drastic hit!

While going from calm to exploding may seem unrealistic, mismanaging your emotions can lead you down this path faster than you might realize. Unfortunately, most of us have had those nights where we lie in bed, thinking about how we went off on something as small as putting away a toy. Those types of moments where we lose it over something little are real-life examples of this happening. As an Empowered Father, learn from these times so that you can do something to keep them from happening again and again.

If you continue to move through life without managing your emotions and running on the negative messages you have received in your life, it is the quality and connection of your relationship that will suffer. The more you engage in this cycle of exploding at small things, the faster it happens the next time if you don't change anything. Managing your emotional experience keeps you from erupting at the small stressors and moves you from a closed to an open mindset in your communication.

Being open while communicating means that you listen to what your children have to say. As you listen, you assess the situation with a calm mind and deal with the problem in a healthy, collaborative, and constructive manner. This isn't easy to do, especially if your children have pushed your buttons repeatedly. To stay open with your communication, do not force your emotional reactions down. Instead, use what they are telling you to benefit your relationship. As long as you keep thinking, you will lower the intensity of your emotions.

If you are struggling to label your emotions, reflect that to your child in an appropriate manner. You can always fall back on a comment such as, "this situation clearly has me confused; please tell me more." Or, if you are struggling to continue positively, you can say, "I'm frustrated enough I need a break; let's get back together in 15 minutes." It would be best if you managed your emotions so they don't throw your communication off course. Managing your emotions allows you to communicate appropriately and builds the balance for your relationship.

**_Impacts on Discipline._** We know there will be times our children break a rule or push the boundaries we have set for them. Disciplining our children is a direct form of communication on how we will deal with this situation. The way we manage our emotions will influence the type of discipline we choose, impacting the relational bank account balance.

The emotions we have influences our perceptions about a situation. While we will look at perception in a later chapter, let's just say that our perceptions impact how we see and interpret a situation or person. Without managing our emotions, these perceptions can become distorted in ways that do not benefit our children and our relationship with them. That's because we will react and intensify the situation beyond what was needed. Let's use a sports analogy to help clarify this.

In the game of football, there are set penalties when specific rules are broken. For example, when a team is called for a false start, they get a five-yard penalty rather than have the person that jumped offsides get ejected. It's easy in this situation to recognize the five-yard penalty as appropriate, whereas an ejection is clearly over the top. Yet, when our perceptions are distorted and emotions are high, we penalize our children far more than what the situation calls for. How often do you find yourself in this situation? What are the consequences of dropping a higher penalty that does not fit the circumstances?

Overreactions with penalties come from the mismanagement of emotions and a failure to see how they are coming into play. When we are not aware of our emotions and frustration levels, we will hand out harsher penalties. We might turn the Legos' situation on the floor from having our children pick them up to a shouting match and using verbal force to get things cleaned up. We may even feel justified because of our frustrations and closed-minded perspective reinforcing our perceptions. This leads to a dramatically larger withdrawal from the relational bank account than was necessary.

Further, our verbal onslaught will likely include strong words, insults, and a tone that conveys anger and fear instead of love. We move from a simple 5-yard penalty to an ejection over a simple rule infraction! These words will take us from encouraging our child to discouraging them, and a discouraged child is more likely to misbehave!

*Impacts on Encouragement.* As a dad, there is no doubt you love and care for your child while wanting the best for them.

However, if you cannot take care of your emotions, this all comes out in the way you encourage or discourage your child. Think back on the last year in your life. Can you think of a time where you were hopeful about something at work or home, only to be met with disappointment? How did you manage that disappointment? Was it in a way that motivated you to try again, or did it put an end to your motivation and hope?

There are times that we tell ourselves we are fine when we are discouraged. We push it down or play it off and believe that we are ready to move on with our lives. If we are not dealing with this appropriately, it will come out through other avenues. Instead of encouraging our children to try harder, keep moving forward, and not give up, we may provide a different message. We deliver the opposite message in our discouraged state by saying life sucks and life will only get you down. Negative emotions can be contagious, even if we do not mean for them to be. Don't let your discouragement bring down your child's enthusiasm. Encourage them because there is already enough discouragement for them to face in their world!

### How Emotions Impact Our Children

Time to look at the second topic, our emotions' direct impact on our children. So far, this chapter's flow has focused on you and how your emotional management could impact your health, behavior, and relationships with your children. This section will widen the focus to include your child's responses and what they are learning from you. Let's start by looking at their inner voice.

***Their Inner Voice.*** We have a voice in our head that keeps a running dialogue about our lives. The things this voice says influence our emotions, thoughts, self-concept, values, and beliefs. As an adult, this voice is influential and strong, even if we have grown familiar with it. However, childhood is where this voice is trained, which comes mostly from others' influence. As fathers, we have a strong effect on the way our children begin to view who they are, how they see the world, and the ways they talk to themselves.

The first part of this chapter asked you about the messages about emotions you got when growing up. The role that you are playing has been switched from when you were a child. Instead of being young and impressionable to other's messages, you are now the one delivering them. The messages you are offering will influence your children as they move through life. If you are still wrestling with emotions and where you stand with them, what messages do you believe you are sending your children?

This is where the difference in knowing where we stand versus where we do not have a profound impact. If we have a more sensitive child who quickly turns to emotions, we need to know what we are communicating to them. We may say that we are okay with feelings and letting our children experience theirs. However, if we are actually uncertain about emotion or feel they are a waste of time, we will deliver that message through our behavior and communication.

We do this through subtle cues or direct messages. Let me share an example. When I was going through school to become a therapist, we discussed a tissue box's role in a session. If a client is crying on the couch and I hand them a tissue box out of concern, what message could I be sending? I may think it was concern and care, whereas the client may see it as I want them to stop crying. This is a mixed message, and it only confuses the situation. What mixed messages might you be sending as a father?

The inner voice of your child will struggle to balance your message if it is consistently mixed. If you tell your children that emotions are okay but then get stern and firmly tell them "quit crying" when they are having a moment, this only creates confusion. They will also pick up on your tone, which feeds the critical side of their inner voice. This leads to a higher volume and level of criticism from their inner voice, leading them to feel shame about their emotions. They may come to see themselves as weak as they attempt to interpret your mixed message.

Being aware of your emotions allows you to deliver a more concise and clear message. You can help your children learn to manage their feelings in ways that keep their inner voice from growing overly critical. Keeping their inner voice from going critical helps keep them from developing a negative self-image of themselves. This has a dramatic impact on how they feel about themselves and live their life.

Mixed messages are not the only way you could be feeding the negativity of their inner voice. When you cannot keep your emotions in check, you might go off with a much larger emotional reaction than the situation needed. Being human means dealing with tough situations even when you are stressed, hungry, and exhausted. If you let yourself jump to a level 10 reaction with your children, you will be left with a choice to make.

You can apologize and reconnect, or you can keep yelling and letting your emotions run the show. Whichever option you choose, just know you will be impacting your child. One of the things that happen when your emotional reaction is more intense than necessary is your use of extreme terms. This is when you use words like always, never, or only. "You *always* do this," "why do you *never* pay attention," or "you *only* think about yourself!"

The more frequently you use these terms with your children, the more their inner voice internalizes them, which leads them to think that is who they are. Unfortunately, you can complicate this further because you might add other words that make this recipe even more dangerous. There's a chance that terms such as lazy, bad, stupid, or manipulative could be added. These are words that leave a bad taste when you are calm and feel connected with your child. However, when you have not managed your emotions, you might feel justified and even good with your emotional eruption, and your children pay the price for your failure to control yourself.

There is a lot of danger in letting these emotional reactions happen. When we use such extreme terms and labels, it tells our children how we feel about them as a person rather than their behavior. We take away their positive actions and focus only on their negatives and deficits. The more we use these words, the more they begin to see themselves in this way. Once they start internalizing this as part of their identity, they are going to start acting accordingly. An adolescent I worked with at a treatment center illustrated this best when he told me, "my parents have always let me know I am the bad child of our family that never listens, so I was just being the rebel I thought I was."

We've covered a lot so far, and you might be wondering how all this connects to emotions and our ability to handle them. If we are not managing our frustration, anger, sadness, stress, and anxieties in respectful and beneficial ways, we are more apt to react and say things that cause a lot of damage.

Remember, you are not just demonstrating for your children how to work with emotions; you are teaching them how to talk to and see themselves. If you are not taking care of yourself and your emotions, you may be sending powerfully destructive messages you did not intend that could have life-altering impacts on your children.

Our lack of emotional regulation will influence how our child sees who they are and how they should behave. This might lead to even more of the behaviors we did not like and *reacted* to as they try to fulfill the role we gave them through our labels. The more often this happens, the more it becomes a deeper pattern in your relationship. This means you will be expending a ton of energy as you work hard to get your relationship back to where you want it, if you can. You can change this cycle by helping them understand their emotional world.

### Labeling Emotions

There is a technique for regulating emotions that we have not worked on yet, and it is the ability to identify and label our emotions. If you grew up with messages that say shove your feelings down because they are not for men, this technique will take some practice. We can experience many different emotions, and the more you have avoided them, the harder they can be to label.

Part of managing and regulating your emotions comes from identifying just what you are feeling and experiencing. Often it is easy to create oversimplified categories for emotions, such as happiness, sadness, and anger. Take the time to expand your awareness and knowledge of your emotional experience, and you will find you take control of the wheel rather than your emotions grabbing it.

Another benefit of labeling is that it can help us put a face on the unknown of our emotional experience. There can be a profound sense of security when we know what we are facing. The more confident we are about labeling our emotions, the less stress and anxiety they will create. Keep in mind, feelings like anger often mask something deeper like fear, embarrassment, or sadness. If we can start identifying most of what we are feeling, we can begin to manage ourselves and respond rather than *react* to situations.

Let's bring this back to how it impacts your children directly. You are their first teacher in life. They will start to learn valuable life skills from you, including how to handle emotions. As your children grow, they will be experiencing a lot of things for the first time. They are inexperienced, young, and uncertain of what they are going through. Sometimes as a father, you know this intuitively, but you may not always think about this in your approach.

Your children are not little adults, even if you wish they were. They do not just know how to manage everything they face in life, no matter their level of intelligence. Managing your emotions is a learning process that takes experience and skills. Professional athletes are amazing at whey do because they work at it. A quarterback knows how to throw the ball, read a defense, and a million different plays because they continuously practice and refine their skills. This process is similar to managing emotions. You must practice it, live it, and continuously learn so you can help your children do the same.

As a father, you need to coach your children on the skills necessary to manage their emotional experience. If you do not have the skills or methods yourself, there is no way you will teach it. Your level of competence in managing emotions is the highest level you will transfer to your children. If you provide them with limited tools, what might be the outcome of that? In essence, you will be asking them to change a flat tire with just a hammer and screwdriver.

One of the crucial tools you need to provide is the ability to label emotions. This allows your children to put a face on what they are going through, which again minimizes the stress and anxiety that comes with experiencing the unknown. You can help them identify their emotional experience in the ways you communicate with them. For example, you could say something like, "you know, if my friend did not pick me for the basketball team in gym class, I would not only be mad, I might also be embarrassed and unsure of how I felt about my friend."

What is going on in a comment like this that is so helpful? You are validating the experience of what they went through and feeling. You also help identify other potential emotions they are experiencing, which allows the child to follow up with questions or more interaction in general. This comment's goal is not to be 100% correct; instead, it is to help them identify what they are experiencing.

Another way to help children label their emotions is by letting them hear us identify ours. We do this with comments such as, "I feel quite upset that the bank did not deposit the refund yet; it seems disrespectful to withhold someone's money like that!" Comments like these do not even need to be directed at anyone in particular. The goal is to help children understand that experiencing emotion is a normal part of being human and that labeling our feelings helps us handle them better.

There is an added benefit to teaching our children how to label their emotions. This benefit is the ability to recognize the emotional experience of others. This has enormous ramifications for their future intimate relationships and friendships. As they grow comfortable with their own experience, they will have the ability to see what others are going through and put themselves in their shoes. It helps them empathize with others, something that is missing in today's world and relationships.

As an Empowered Father, seek to teach your children how to label their emotions and recognize others' emotional experiences. There is not much benefit in teaching them to hide from their experience or the feelings of others. Helping children out with their emotions adds deposits to the relational bank account and teaches them how to make deposits in other important relational bank accounts in their lives.

## Final Thoughts

Emotions are a complicated topic. Many of us have grown up being taught to avoid them because they are pointless. If this is your view, I challenge you to look at why you believe this is the case. What would happen if you began to open your world to your emotional experience? How would allowing yourself to experience emotions help you regulate them? What could happen if you provide your children with a different message about emotions than the one you received?

We need more than just rational thought to navigate our lives. If we are too logical and avoid emotions, we will come off as Spock, but without all the intergalactic travel and knowledge. This means we are not necessarily the ones people want to talk to or come to for support. How would this come into play with your children? If they can't come to us, who will they go to? What do you need to do more of, and what needs to change about emotions so you can build a relationship that encourages your child to come to you?

It takes time, patience, persistence, humility, and self-compassion to re-write deeply entrenched beliefs like those we have about emotions. Each day try and improve over the day before. Often, as men, we try to handle our feelings in the same way each time. If something is not working, have the courage and humility to try something else. Do more of what is working and less of what is not; just make sure you are honest with yourself about whether or not what you are doing is truly working!

Interacting with your children on a deep, emotional level can create a connection more robust than anything previously experienced. It will bring the relational bank account to life for you. You will sense it, feel it, and know when there have been deposits or withdrawals. Emotions are not pointless, and they do not make you less of a man. They are for all humans to experience, and they help guide us in life while fostering deeper levels of connection with others. Take the time necessary to get to know your emotional side. You might be surprised how much the world around you opens up and how much deeper your connection with your family gets!

# | 6 |

# Control

This chapter covers the particularly tricky and powerful topic of control, which is a word in our culture that has come to have a more negative connotation than it deserves. The way we define this word for ourselves will impact our roles as a man, partner, and father. It influences how we treat our children while we manage our own behavior. Unfortunately, the negative examples of males using control to gain power throughout history have distorted our views. As a dad, a key part of your success will be assessing and understanding what control means to you.

You can thank the primitive parts of our brains for the way we act around control. Our brains often interpret the threat of losing control as life or death, which triggers old survival patterns. This made a ton of sense when a saber-tooth tiger would chase our ancestors, but is way out of place when our three-year-old won't pick up their socks!

The need to feel control is embedded deep in every human being, which is how marketers have made a killing off of us. Think about satellite providers who offer you 500 channels, of which you will probably watch five to ten channels consistently. You may never touch all the channels, but it is sure cool knowing you could if you wanted to! We like to feel in control, and this does not change as a father.

When control is balanced in our homes, parents and children will have a fair say, and a state of harmony is reached. Let's be clear, that does not mean children have equal status as parents. Rather, it means everyone can have their needs for control acknowledged and their voices heard. When chaos occurs in our homes, it usually comes from someone fighting for their piece of the control pie. When we find a way to share this pie, the chaos naturally goes down in intensity.

If you are the type of man who likes to have the say in all that goes on, having children will be one of the biggest threats to your sense of control. We must explore our beliefs about control if we want to be the most effective father we can be. A simple fishing metaphor might help make this clearer.

## Fishing and Control

Going fishing was one of the big things my family would do together. I learned many life lessons from my father and brother standing on the shore and casting a line into the water. One lesson that sticks out to me was about the power of control and keeping it in balance, and it was taught to me with fishing line.

Our favorite fish to catch was smallmouth bass, which we caught by letting a jig sink to the bottom slowly while it flowed with the current. As I learned how to fish with this technique, my father taught me about the line's tension. He mentioned that the best chance of catching a fish came when there was the right balance of tension on your fishing line.

He had me keep the reel open on one cast, allowing the line to flow out freely and pool in the water just feet from where we were standing. In a few moments, the line out furthest began to twitch in a way that meant a fish was taking the jig. At this point, I did what any fisherman is taught to do and attempted to set the hook. However, I soon ran into a problem. With all the line pooled in the water, lifting the pole did not provide the necessary pressure on the line. I was forced to reel in as fast as I could for a few moments before I could set the hook again. Of course, by then, the fish was gone.

Seeing my frustration at losing the fish, my father taught me the first part of the lesson about control. He let me know that if there is too much line out, you can't always pull it back in and get the tension you need to catch the fish. Too much slack gives the fish too much freedom. Flustered and not overly open to the lesson at that point, I cast my line again to catch the fish that got away.

This time I decided to try a new plan, which I'm sure my father was expecting. Instead of letting the line flow freely, I decided to keep the line firm constantly. I felt a sense of pride as I could feel the current pull on the jig through the line. It only took a few moments before I felt that exciting pull on the line. I knew this time the fish was mine, and I quickly set the hook.

My excitement soon turned to frustration again as the fish got off the hook. How could this be? My line had no slack, and I had been diligent in keeping it as firm as I could. Again, my father could see the unhappiness on my face, and he expressed to me the second part of the lesson. He taught me that if the line is kept too tight and firm, it will pull the hook right out of the fish's mouth. This leaves us as empty hooked as letting all the line out. Too much slack or tension gave the fish the opportunity it needed to escape while allowing my levels of frustration to rise.

On the third cast, my dad helped me teach me what the right balance of tension and slack looked and felt like. The line had a slight curl pattern to it as it laid on the water, and only a couple turns of the reel would tighten it back up. This time when the fish bit and I set the hook, something different happened. The fish stayed on the line! While I wish I could say I caught a trophy, I was good with at least being able to reel in a fish. I cast a few more times and was able to bring in a fish this way several more times.

After more casts, something else happened. I was able to get a fish on the line with this delicate balance of tension and slack, feeling unstoppable from the numerous fish I had already reeled in. This particular fish did not make it to shore, though; it got off the line. I looked at my dad, confused at what happened, and this was when he gave me the third lesson on control. Even if we keep ourselves balanced, we cannot control the other part of the equation: the fish. All I could control is what I did with the line and reel, and the other variables in the situation were out of my control.

While it may seem overly simple, this fishing story teaches us a lot about control and fathering. The more our line is slacked, the less control we have. This is the same as being too flexible with control and our children, making it harder for us to reel it in when we need to! If we keep the line too tight, we limit our options and end up with less control. This is when we try to maintain control and enforce it strictly with our children. This leads to children fighting back to get their control back, and we lose ours.

When we keep the line just right, we have a much better chance of bringing the fish in. This is when we balance the needs for control in the home, provide a consistent structure and enforce it, and regularly build our relationship with our children. For this to happen, we need to understand our views on control. To help with this, let's look at how control influences the roles we play in life.

### Control and the Roles We Play

We wear a lot of different hats in our lives. We can be a son, husband, partner, father, professional, student, soldier, uncle, nephew, and on and on. We are never just a single role in our life, even if that would simplify things! We are going to look at control within the context of our roles as men and fathers.

Control is the sense that different elements of your life are under your power or influence, which gives you a say in what might happen. Balancing control in our roles can be a difficult process. Our experiences help shape our beliefs about control and what we are willing to do to hold onto it. If we have had relationships in the past where we have been hurt and trust has been abused, we are more likely to hoard control in future relationships.

We become rigid to avoid future pain and hurt, without realizing the opposite tends to happen, and we create more pain and hurt for others and ourselves. The more we grasp to control, the more we forget about others and what we might do to them. How would this impact your role as a father?

Our views on control influence our behavior as we interact with our children. The more rigid we are, the less patience we have and more hesitant we'll be to grant our children freedom. It should be no surprise, but beliefs about control start when we were being raised. While not set in stone, you have behavior patterns from these beliefs that started in your past.

If you grew up in a home where a parent hoarded control, you might have felt like their puppet with a starved need of control. When old enough to begin making your own decisions and having your own views on life, you might have binged on it with all your might. If we have gone through a control famine for years and then it suddenly becomes available on the menu, we like to indulge like there is no tomorrow!

Not having any control comes with insecurity, so when we get a taste of control, we are likely to fight harder to keep it. We become more rigid and set in our ways. As fathers, this leads us to a fork in the road with no guarantee which way we will go. To help you decide, let's see where the different forks lead.

The left fork is where we vow not to starve our children of control, so we let them have too much. We give in to their wants and honor nearly every one of their requests and decisions. We do not want to look like an evil, power-hungry leader, so we step back to prevent hoarding control from our children. This gives us a false sense of control, and it typically comes around to get us once we decide to reel everything back in. The longer we let our children run the show, the less they see us as authority figures. When this happens, we will struggle to enforce the structure and boundaries in our home. There is too much slack on the fishing line if we head down this fork!

The fork on the right leads to the opposite end of this spectrum. These are the parents that continue the control hoarding cycle in their own family. Any thinking done in the family is done by the one with the control, not by the children. Rules are firm with no room for exceptions or minimal changes with the child's development. Any statement or action by our children that is opposite of our thoughts is seen as a threat and treated as such. Small misbehaviors and situations go from molehills to mountains. There is too much tension on the fishing line.

These reactions are why we need to be aware of our views on control and how they impact our children and us. When we get rigid in our beliefs, we see only the extreme options on the left or right instead of other paths we can choose. These different paths help bring a better balance for control in our relationships with our children.

Let's face it, children bring an element of chaos with them. A military father I worked with said it best when he stated, "the army prepared me to disarm a bomb, but they did nothing to train me on how to disarm a two-year-old!" This is why we need the flexibility to achieve the delicate balance of slack and tension on the line. The more rigid we are, the more we will fight for control. If we are too flexible, we will hardly ever be in control. The way that balance looks will be different for everyone, and that is fine. All that matters is finding the balance that works for you.

You need to understand what control means to you in your role of being a man. We get our ideas about control from sources that include the men in our lives growing up, the media we indulge in, and reinforcements to our behavior we received in social settings. The more we understand control and being a man, the better we will identify our beliefs as a father.

Every human on Earth wants some morsel of control as it is an inherent need we all have. For some, control has become a life or death need, and they will hold onto it for dear life. If having control for you has been starved, it will move from a need into I-absolutely-must-have-it-or-the-world-will-end territory!

Okay, while that is slightly exaggerated, there is such thing as needs becoming absolute necessities. When your need for control turns into an absolute necessity, you develop tunnel vision and see only what you are losing. You become defensive, take things personally, lash out, yell, or do something extreme to get control back. Sounds like a two-year-old having a tantrum, right? Well, that's because that's what tantrums are! Your children want control, just like you, and if you have an adult tantrum, you increase the chances of them having one too.

Too much rigidity in relationships doesn't work. Relationships are a delicate balance of give and take. For example, in the early years, your child will do more taking than giving while you do a lot of the giving without much in return. As the years move on, this should move towards a more balanced state, and some children make this process easier than others.

A healthy balance of control means sharing it with our children. Remember, the more rigid we become, the more likely we are to see an eruption between our children and us. Flexibility is required, though, be careful not to provide too much control that your child can't handle it all. Take the time to figure out what control you can give up if you have been too rigid. If you are too flexible, think about where you can give control back.

To find a healthy balance of control, take the time to understand what it means to you and where you are willing to let some go, or reel it in, if necessary. Many of the fights we get into with our children are over each person trying to meet their needs for control. Remember to focus on what is in your control rather than what is not!

### What is in Our Control?

One of the hard parts is knowing what is actually within our control. Crazy right? An Empowered Father recognizes that their behavior and how they respond to situations are in their control. We may not have control over the outcome, but we do have the choice of what behavior and actions we take—trying to control the outcome or what someone else does will only lead to struggle and disconnect.

If you try to force your child to do something to get the outcome you want, it will come at a price. Your moments of having a false sense of control blinds you from the major withdrawals you are making from the relational bank account. Also, your upset child will be less likely to do what you ask for in the future. This usually leads to threats and verbal outbursts on your part to get what you want, and just like that, you have a negative power cycle in your relationship.

While you cannot control what your children do, you can positively influence them, which is far more effective in the long-term. Keeping your behavior and responses in control is how you can positively influence your environment and create more of what you want to see. This creates a climate of respecting the choices and autonomy for you and your child while strengthening the relationship.

Exercising your control in influential ways leads to better outcomes, including maintaining your child's integrity and your relational bank account's balance. Instead of forcing your child out of *reaction*, you will take a proactive approach that helps you remain calm and collected. This will be more effective with a consistent structure already in place. You can draw on the structure to help you stay calm and in control because you have something to fall back on other than *reacting*.

For some, proactive approaches may not seem like enough. If you want something done and since you are the father, it better get done now! Reacting with anything other than threats seems soft and that you are giving the power to your child. I would challenge you to think about whether the power method truly keeps you in control in a way that maintains trust, safety, and connection with your child. Will it help you build the relationship you want to have with your child in the future?

You can still be an authority figure without relying on just the power of your position. You can lead with the power of the relationship and build your children up. It is possible to share control and still maintain structure and order in the home. You do not have to erupt at every trivial misbehavior of your child just to keep your sense of control.

If you see a majority of your child's behaviors as attempts to take your control, you will be *reactive* because you perceive them as a threat. The more you engage from a *reactive* view, the more out of control you actually are. Instead of being proactive and maximizing your options to maintain control and find solutions, you react and limit the positive outcomes while decreasing your control levels. Part of why you may be overly *reactive* has to deal with the concept of respect.

### Control and Respect

Respect is a value that has a close connection to fatherhood, even if it can be finicky in nature! It can time a long time for respect to build up and only a couple of adverse incidents to tear it down. What does respect have to do with our need for control? How connected are the two?

The more in control we are of ourselves, the more likely we are to engage with our children respectfully. When we can see the situation objectively and respond instead of *react*, we are also treating ourselves with respect. Staying in control keeps our relational bank account strong and our actions respectful as we know when to stay in or step out of a given situation.

Showing this type of respect for ourselves also impacts

our children as we treat them the same. Approaching situations with our children respectfully and productively keeps the integrity of our child untarnished. We will be using empathy because we recognize that we do not like to be steamrolled for our mistakes, so we will not do this to our children. Responding with empathy shows our children respect for who they are as individuals while reaffirming our love and care for them.

Fathering this way also demonstrates respect for the relationship we have with our child. It shows our child that we care for this moment and the future of our relationship. This helps stabilize the floor beneath our child's feet, so they do not have to fear where they stand. We need to respect who they are as unique individuals and the connection we share. This eliminates insecurity and fear, two common reasons for misbehavior!

When you lose control and use power methods to get your point across and teach a lesson, you do not show your children respect. You are going against how respect develops in a relationship. Respect needs to be earned by both the father and the child. When you lose control and draw on authority and power, you are neglecting respect.

The father, who relies only on power and authority, demands respect. Unfortunately, the more respect gets demanded, the less there is available. When a lack of respect gets reciprocated, this fuels the dad's power trip, which leads to more disrespect and use of power. These fathers begin to see their children as disrespectful, entitled, out of control, and manipulative. Ironically, they are getting back what they gave in the first place. If we do not treat our children with respect, why in the world would they give it back?

As an Empowered Father, move past demanding respect. Take the time and steps necessary to earn your child's respect, which starts by showing them respect. Father knowing that respect is a two-way street and drawing on power and authority turns that street into a dead-end. One powerful way to show respect to our children is to help them learn to manage their need for control.

### Control and Our Children

It is probably not too hard to believe that your children want control of their lives as much as we wish that for ours. Children are experts at finding new and creative ways to get control of their environment. Some children start by asking calmly for what they want, making it easier for us dads to keep ourselves in control. In fact, we might even feel a sense of pride when our children manage their desires for control in such a healthy and respectful way.

However, when we deny their request, our children are likely to use other methods to try and get control back. Some of their ways will make us scratch our heads or bring out the worst in us. They may backtalk you or cross their arms firmly when you ask them to get something done. You might hear foot stomps down the hallway after they have run out of the room and slammed the door for emphasis. They do this to let you know they are not on board with your ideas.

Children know how to up the ante when there is a public audience. They can't slam the door in a store, so instead, they raise their voice, roll around on the ground screaming and crying and punching the floor. It puts us in a strange predicament as we get to father with an audience. It gets even more fun at restaurants when our children figure out how good chicken nuggets are as missiles when they are mad. Our children seek to gain control in any way that they can, even if they have to go ballistic to get it.

These moments test us on managing our own control, and it seems our children get this. It is almost as if every child has coded in their brains that the more out of control they get us, the more power they get in the situation. This means it does not matter what extremes they need to go to; they'll eventually get what they need. This is how the cycle of control struggles begins.

*Control Struggles.* There are several options for what we can do when it comes to our children and their control needs. We can try to smash that need to keep our needs satisfied, give in to their behavior, or foster it in healthy ways. Fathers who use the power method are seeking to smash this need. They use insults, threats, and force to keep the child acting the way they believe they should. Unfortunately, these fathers tend to find over time that they are not quelling these struggles for control. Instead, they are leading themselves and their child down a dangerous path that includes more battles.

Control struggles can happen in any type of relationship. When you bring two different people together, their views and needs will eventually clash, which sometimes leads to a control struggle. Use the power method for many years sets us up for hard times when the adolescent years arrive. The results we see with younger children giving in can fool us into believing it is an effective method. Unfortunately, we will see the fruits of our labors when they reach adolescence.

To children, when control struggles have been standard practice in the relationship, their goal is to find new ways to satisfy their starved need for control. When younger, they do things like having a fit in the middle of the store or throwing chicken nuggets at us. These are not that big of a deal since they are more annoying behaviors rather than risky. However, as the child grows, the risks they take to get control do become more dangerous.

If their need for control has been deprived long enough, adolescents will do extreme things like steal the car, not eat or purge what they do, self-harm, try alcohol and drugs, have unprotected sex, run away from home, commit a crime, skip school, or attempt to commit suicide. When we have taken control from our children throughout their lives, we push them into a corner. Just as a dog will do whatever it needs to get out, so will our children. They will grab any form of control possible, even if it is incredibly dangerous.

Fathering only with the power method to curb our children's control-seeking behavior opens our future up to pain and heartache. Our children will be more likely to seek out the things we do not want, or that could be lethal. If we believe we should have all the power in the relationship, our relational bank account will deplete rapidly. Take it to the extreme and we may lose our child in ways that we can never have them back. These are outcomes that wait for us if we choose to smash their need for control. What might happen if we try giving in instead?

***Giving In.*** Let's face it, when our children are kicking and screaming in the checkout lane, giving in seems like the easiest thing to do to get control back of our child and the situation quickly. It gives us a false sense of being in control because we feel we chose to provide them with what they wanted willingly rather than *reacting* to their behavior. In reality, it is not control, and it is merely putting the control in our child's hands rather than ours.

Doing this repeatedly will lead to some troubles down the road. Any time we try to assert ourselves, a program starts to run in our child's head. This program remembers the times that the child wanted something and their father initially said no, but gave in to their kicking and screaming. This program understands that 99 no's and one yes is still a yes. This teaches the child that any want should be seen as a detrimental need and to act accordingly. As fathers, we sometimes reply with the button-pushing two-letter word, no.

When our child hears the word no, that program reinforces the belief that 99 no's and one yes is still a yes, so keep pushing! They are ready to fight for that one thing because they feel their control is slipping. Since they were able to get their way previously through tantrums, they do it again and again. If we choose to continue giving in, we will be putting ourselves in a lose-win situation. The father loses, and the child wins, which is not an ideal place to be.

As our children grow older, these struggles continue and

solidify the lose-win outcomes in the relationship. When this happens, our child may grow up to be entitled, wanting whatever they want when they want it without concern for the cost to others. Since their father has given in time and time again, there have been no lessons on boundaries, gratitude, or working for anything. When the father decides to try and take a stand, the child quickly overpowers them to repeat the cycle. In terms of the fishing metaphor, too much slack on the line has given too much power to the child.

Giving in can move from being a temporary solution to a situation to a downward spiral of complete chaos. Our children gain too much control that they are not mature enough to wield. Instead of coaching our children about finding a balance with their need for control, we have just given them all the power. That creates quite a dilemma for us when we need to be a father and handle a situation. It will be hard to do since all the power is with the child!

Control is as slippery as trying to catch a fish. It can quickly go from in our possession to entirely out of our hands. While it may seem that we are doomed to be in a lose-win situation, that is not the case. We can help our children learn to manage control by coaching them through the responsibilities of wielding that power while maintaining our own control.

*Meeting Control Needs.* Fostering healthy control balances with our children requires us to let go of some of the control we do not need. Empowered Fathers identify ways to meet their child's needs for control through appropriate doses that help the child learn how to manage that power and responsibility.

We do not need to control every step or detail of our child's life. If they want to put their left shoe on first instead of the right one, is that really a big deal? Our job is not to dictate what they do with their control. Instead, our task is to help them learn how to manage it to make their own decisions. When we dictate what they do, we smash their sense of control and typically create more of the behavior we do not want to see. We are putting ourselves in a lose-win situation by choice if we do this.

As fathers, we need to have the ability to look at situations objectively. When our children ask for something, attempt to make their own decisions, or try something they wanted out, we need to know where we can let go of some control. We may disagree with some of what they want to do, but we can still decide if there is control we can give up or if it is worth taking a stand.

Remember, our children have the same need for control that we do. When we are willing to let go of every detail and focus only on the important ones, we can put ourselves in a win-win situation by maintaining our control and our child's as well. So, what are some ways we can do this?

*Options*

A simple and effective technique is to provide options for our children. It is as simple as offering A or B options, such as a hot dog (A) or sandwich (B) for lunch. When we provide options, we are not dictating our child's response and taking their control. Instead, we provide an opportunity for them to have control and move our relationship into win-win territory.

Providing various options allows us to maintain control of the overall goal while giving our children the freedom to decide how they will move forward. In the example of hot dogs or sandwiches for lunch, the only outcome we want is for our child to eat. Providing options allows our child to fulfill their need for control by selecting what they will eat, making our job that much easier!

Of course, if you provide only two options, there is a high chance you will hear a third option, if not a fourth. Listen to them and see this as the child attempting to learn how to make decisions and think for themselves. Listening to the options our child provides is incredibly validating to them. Chances are they are predicting you are not going to listen and will shut them down immediately.

Listening and validating lets your child know you have heard them and acknowledge their ideas. You may have to decline their option this time, but you can still leave the door open to it in the future. This is done through a comment like, "wow, filet mignon would be great for lunch today if only we had it! We'll have to see what we can do about that another day. Will it be hot dogs or sandwiches for today?"

Keep in mind that validating their idea is not the same as taking it. If it is a no, we can leave it at that or express when that idea might happen in the future. What about if your child provides an option you like and is doable? You do not have to say no just because it wasn't one of your options. If you are good with it, who not go with it? You increase your child's confidence in themselves to think and make decisions, which is very important. Further, the relational bank account gets a big deposit, and you come off as a cool dad rather than an opponent. That is what you call a win-win-winning-it-all situation!

*Granting Autonomy*

Fathers I have worked with have shared many creative ways to balance their needs with their child's needs for control. When discussing chores or jobs around the house, some dads provide a list of things that need to get done and have the children sign up for them. Others give a list of jobs that need to be done by each child, one for every day of the week. On this list, two of the seven slots are left blank to allow the child a chance to choose their job for those days.

You might be wondering what to do when these chores are not completed. Some of the dads I've worked with have a list of consequences on the fridge for just this situation. The child is provided with a chance to pick one, and if they fail to do so, the parent gets to decide. Clever, right? Other fathers work with their children on determining what consequences to put in place for a failure to complete chores. It might surprise you how often children come up with more severe consequences than what we would have!

Overall, when we maintain our sense of control and fulfill this need, we help foster healthy ways for our children to manage their needs around control. This helps us keep our relational bank account green, especially since there will be fewer control struggles. It's essential to understand why your ability to manage yourself when faced with situations that challenge your desired levels of control is crucial, so let's check that out.

### Control and Managing Ourselves

Managing ourselves is more than taking care of our thoughts and emotions. It is knowing what we can give up and what needs to be held onto. Let's face it; no one likes a backseat driver or a micromanager. Yet, when we feel the need to assert our control over our children, that is the exact type of father we become.

We do this by attempting to guide our children through unsolicited advice, fix the situation for them, or putting down our foot. We got from the Empowered Father approach of being a teacher, mentor, and coach and turn into a micro-managing boss. It's no wonder our children push back against this; it's precisely what we do when we feel micromanaged!

When we talk about managing ourselves, it is the ability and willingness to understand our needs around control. We must identify where we can let some go so we can create win-win situations. I have heard a lot of dads use the game of tug-of-war as a metaphor for fathering. There are times it does fit, especially when our needs differ from our child's. Keep in mind that no one truly wins when it comes to control struggles with your child, which is why we must learn to manage ourselves.

We will manage ourselves when we understand the only thing we can truly control is ourselves and how we respond. Our children will provide us a lot of invitations to engage in a control struggle. When we maintain our control, we know that we do not have to accept every invitation. We willingly decline to engage in every control struggle, which has powerful long-term benefits.

Throughout your children's lives, they will face many different thought and value systems about who they should be and how they should live. Some you will be okay with; others will be against your family value system. If you have accepted every control struggle invitation through their life, your voice becomes less important because they are worn down and choose not to hear it anymore. They know what to expect and that it will not be in their favor. They feel disconnected from you because your repeated control struggles have depleted the relational bank account.

If you have managed yourself and accepted invitations only when it was vital, something different happens instead of engaging in every power struggle. Our voice is more genuine and respected by our child. They know something is different because we have chosen to speak up. The communication chapter will help you speak up in a way that respects your child's integrity and character. Empowered Fathers know that when they accept these invitations, going in with force and volume is not going to help. Seek to understand before providing your viewpoint.

We want our words to have power and influence when we need them to. Young children who have grown up in a home where they are always yelled at learn to tune out our voice and move on with their lives. We need to be mindful of when we are attempting to voice control more than usual to ensure that it is at the times that are truly warranted. Remember, we need to find the balance of just enough tension on the fishing line!

## Final Thoughts

If we are always pulling on the rope in a tug-of-war game over control with our children, it becomes familiar to them. That is what they expect in the relationship and from our behavior. This is why we need to choose when we are going to step in. If we are getting in control struggles over which shoe goes on first, how they should wash and style their hair, or any one of a million other small things, this becomes the norm. They expect to get in a fight with us and react as if on auto-pilot.

However, if we learn ways to help our children meet their control needs, our relationship looks a lot different than a game of tug-of-war. Respect strengthens our bonds, and they trust us as we let them learn to make decisions. They know we are here to help teach them and listen, which is useful when dealing with pressures for underage drinking, sexual activity, drugs, academics, and everything else that comes with adolescence. We need our voice to be heard at those critical times, and it will when we have managed ourselves over time.

It will be up to you as a father to decide how you will approach control with your children. Be aware of the types of control struggles you might engage in with your children frequently. If you find yourself engaging in a control struggle over small things like what pair of socks they are wearing, it is time for self-reflection.

Think about what you are trying to accomplish at that moment and if it is as vital as you think it is. If it isn't, what can you let go of? Learn the cues that let you know you are getting pulled into a control struggle. If we learn our triggers, which are usually related to our values, we can stop it before it has a chance to cause destruction. Remember, every control struggle you engage in will be a big withdrawal!

When it comes to your views on control, take the time to assess these views. Look for patterns of rigidity in your thinking and behavior, or if you need to tighten up and reduce the slack. Remember, fatherhood is a journey where there is always room to grow, learn, and change. Check the tension on your line and balance your needs for control with your child. The future relationship you have with your children with thank you for it!

# | 7 |

# Perception: A New Way to See Fatherhood

Why are we so fascinated by magicians and illusions? Why do we question what's possible when we see their tricks? Magicians and illusionists entertain us because they play with our sense of reality. We start to question what is real and what is magic. Their card tricks and disappearing acts throw our brains for a loop as we try to figure out how they are doing what we are seeing. This is a simple way to see how our sense of reality comes from how we perceive the world. Perception is a powerful force in our lives, and while magicians are fun to watch, you might be wondering what this has to do with fatherhood. Good question!

We can use our perceptions to strengthen our relationships with our children or distort and weaken our connection. It is up to you to get in touch with how you perceive and make meaning out of your world. The reason is that your perceptions also influence how you will look and treat your children. Let's take a quick look at how that can happen.

### Your Mental Image of Your Children

When you became a father, you started to have hopes and dreams for your children. You probably started to imagine what they would do, who they will become, and what they will accomplish in their lives. While there is nothing wrong with this, you need to be mindful of how you imagine the future. Keeping your expectations grounded in reality helps keep your perceptions accurate. However, there is another side to this.

Sometimes when imaging the future, we build up an image of the perfect child. We know they will behave better than any other child in the world. They are going to achieve more than anything else the world has seen before. We think we will never fight or argue with our child. Chances are they will not make a lot of mistakes, and the ones they do will not be catastrophic and merely an anomaly. Yes, these statements are exaggerated; however, you might be surprised how many parents do this. This mental picture intensifies our struggles when our child misbehaves, makes mistakes, or has school troubles.

How does perception influence us and our behavior like this? From our perceptions, we make interpretations to create meaning and conclusions. These interpretations are what we use to decide how we will respond to a situation. Faulty or grandiose perceptions lead to incorrect interpretations, which means an inappropriate response on our part. Let's put this into the context of fatherhood.

Our interpretation of our child's behavior is influenced by the perceptions we have of them. When the perfect child in our mind does not align with the reality of who our child is, our perception of them can change. We may choose to continue holding them to a high and unrealistic standard to get them to fit the image. We can also flip that image in our head completely and see nothing more than a manipulative child. Our perception changes so much that we interpret their behavior and character in different ways. This can put the relationship on shaky ground.

To demonstrate this point more, let's talk about illusions. There are examples of images where your first look reveals one thing, but the longer you look, the more the picture changes. Our perception acts as a filter, locking in on one part of the image rather than seeing it all. The same is true for your children. There are times we lock in on certain things, like misbehavior, and start to label our children. You can define and label them by behavior, or take a broader look and see the whole picture. The choice is yours; make sure you think it through!

**Perception and Interpretation**

So, let's rewind a little bit. As a dad, you have a unique way that you look at your world and your children. It would be best if you got to know it because, let's face it, sometimes the way our children behave annoys us. They poke us over and over, try to pull tablets or phones out of our hands, knock glasses of water over, scream, jump, making insane sounds, and the list is endless. If you have a picture in your head of what your child should be and it does not align with who they are in any way, your perception will lock in on the discrepancies. Remember, what you choose to focus your perceptions on influences the interpretations you make and how you will respond.

The more we focus on the discrepancies, the more distorted our perception becomes. As fathers, the more we fix our perception on the same thing repeatedly, the more it influences our interpretations. There is a danger in this because our behavior, which is how we treat our child, is influenced by the interpretation we make of the situation. If your perception is distorted, your interpretation will not be accurate, and your behavior will not align with the situation. Your perception acts as the filter that leads you to make conclusions and react based on only what you have allowed through the filter.

Many of us do not want to believe that we have pigeonholed our children into these tight categories. Our brains are wired to categorize our world, which includes people and our views of them. So, if while reading this, you recognize some of this applies to you, don't guilt or shame yourself. Instead, realize it is normal, and now you know you have the ability to make changes. It is worthwhile to address the image we have in our head of our child and challenge or reinforce it if necessary.

A meaningful way to decide if you need to challenge or reinforce is getting to know your child on a deep level. This happens when you spend time together talking about their likes and dislikes. It also comes when you get to know what is developmentally appropriate for your child. Many dads view their children as little adults without giving them the benefit of the doubt that they are just a child. Sometimes it's an eye-opening experience when we learn what our child should be doing according to child development rather than our expectations. So, how does our perception influence behavior? Let's find out!

### Perception and Behavior

Children are always doing something, some behaviors that we like, some we dislike, and others that are just plain bizarre and amaze us. One thing to keep in mind with children is that all their behavior is purposeful. This means they try to accomplish something with their behavior, even if it doesn't make sense to us. Our children are learning to navigate the world around them, which is usually done through trial-and-error.

Just as we have our perceptions, our children are beginning to shape their own about themselves and of us as their father. One of the ways this perception forms is through our responses to their behavior. If we habitually explode or reply sarcastically to their behavior, it skews their perception of us. We react to their actions in these ways because of our perception and not understanding what they are attempting to accomplish. When we *react* in a counterproductive way to what we want to achieve, we are also impacting the image they have of us.

We need to widen our lenses and realize that our child's behavior falls into more categories than good or bad. Recognize your child's behavior for what it is, a way to communicate about getting their needs met. I worked with a dad who said it worked for him to approach the situation like a detective game where he has to solve the mystery of what his child is expressing. He said this helped him see the behavior as something more than just good or bad, which was a massive change for him, his child, and their relationship.

This father talked a lot at the beginning of our class about how annoying his son could be when they were in the same room. He would jump on the couch, yelling and poking him one minute before suddenly he would be in his bedroom crying. The father stated this frustrated him, and he started to perceive his child as overly emotional, bouncing from an extreme high to an extreme low. While his son's behavior confused him, what hurt him most was how he reacted to his child.

He said his voice went up in volume and intensity when his child acted strangely. There were times he would go into the bedroom and tell his son to strap on his boots and be a man instead of a whiner. He saw his child as weak, which meant his son would grow into a weak man and not make it in the world. This father expressed that his perceptions and interpretations were pigeon-holing his son into this awful corner.

To address that, he began to play the detective game. Instead of yelling, he would say calmly, "I wonder if there is something you want from me." The child began to act differently as his father changed his response to the behavior. This child only wanted his dad's attention and would go to extremes to get it. Negative attention was still better than nothing!

It was a harsh realization for the dad, but one that allowed him to change the cycle. This dad's story illustrates the power of perception and how it impacts our responses. Be cautious about your perceptions of your child's behavior; it could lead to missed opportunities for connection and begin the dangerous practice of labeling our children.

### The Power of Labels

One way perception gets tricky comes when our behaviors and responses influence our child's perceptions of themselves. A particularly powerful way that we impact their perceptions is the labels we use. Labels can be a two-edged sword that helps create confidence and self-esteem or takes the wind right out of our child's sails. If, as an Empowered Father, you choose to use labels, make sure they are ones that will build up your child's sense of self-worth rather than tear them down.

*Positive Labels.* Positive, realistic labels have a way of helping your child come to see themselves as having worth and value. If your child spends all afternoon working on a project that has been giving them problems, you have a window to do something powerful. When they show you the finished project, you have a chance to respond in an empowering way. You could use a statement such as, "wow, you worked hard on this and persevered when things were not going your way, and now you have the project just the way you wanted," to build them up. Does a comment like that seem like a big deal? Let's see what it does in terms of positive labels.

When we respond with a comment like that, the child hears they are hard-working, capable, and able to persevere.

Also, since the statement is specific rather than generic such as "you're the smartest child in the world," the labels are realistic and observable. The project that your child created is evidence of the effort and capability you are pointing out. Your child will begin to see they do have a hard-work ethic, that they can persevere, and they are capable.

There are times that we go into autopilot and say things like "that is the greatest," "you are the funniest kid ever," "you are the smartest," or "no one will ever beat you, champ!" These labels may sound positive, but they also come with a hint of judgment and are based on generalizations rather than specific behaviors. The broader the terms we use, the less realistic they become. The less realistic they become, the more pressure our children feel, and the more likely they are to develop a false sense of self.

Your labels need to be positive and realistic to the child to help them develop a healthy sense of self. I once had parents in my therapy office say they did not understand why their child was so depressed over getting a B+ on a test. When they asked their son, he said, "you always said I was the smartest, but now I know I'm not, I'm dumb and a failure." This child's world crumbled when there was evidence to show these grand statements about him were not true. That is why our labels need to be positive and realistic. Our labels help them build a more accurate picture of who they are and what they can continue to become.

One trick that can help you keep your labels positive and realistic is to look for specific things to point out. If your preschooler hands you a piece of art, resist the temptation to say, "wow, you are the most creative child ever!" Instead, go for specifics by commenting, "Wow, look at all the colors you used and all those curvy lines! Look at that; you used one, two, three, four different colors! It takes creativity to put something like that together!"

Responding with specific feedback communicates several important things to our child. It lets them know they are worth our time as we stop what we are doing to focus on them. It builds the relational bank account and the positive perception of self for our children. We provide realistic expectations for our child and their abilities rather than create undue stress and pressure to perform and reach general labels' unrealistic expectations. We want to avoid that stress and pressure, as it will lead our child to want to please us rather than focus on their own efforts in developing their identity.

Positive and realistic labels have a way of providing our children with reassurance and security. We are not placing negative judgment on them. We are realistic, specific, and supportive rather than grandiose in our feedback. This helps them create a healthy foundation to build their sense of self while eliminating unnecessary stress.

As Empowered Fathers, we want our children to take pride in themselves. That begins when we provide them with positive and realistic labels that are true to their character rather than an impossible measuring stick of who they should be. That is in complete contrast to the mis-power that negative labels can have.

**Negative Labels.** We have seen the power of positive and

realistic labels. Not it's time to consider negative labels and their mis-power. I call it mis-power because negative labels are incredibly powerful and have a lot of influence over how our child sees themselves. However, it is mis-power because it can tear our child apart and creates a negatively biased perspective of themselves.

Let's go back to the example of your child working on a project all day because of the trouble it was giving them. We saw what a positive and realistic response could do to provide positive labels. So, what might a comment be that would lead to negative labels? Before we get to one, I want to mention that these types of comments are easy to fall into, especially if you tend to be more sarcastic. Once you read the example, I think you will see what I mean.

A response that could create negative labels sounds something like, "wow, it only took you *all* afternoon to get that done. I'm pretty sure your sister got all her homework done in that time." So, what is different about this type of response? Have you caught yourself ever starting a statement off with a sarcastic remark like, "it only took you *all* afternoon to get that done?" Be honest, because let's face it, most of us have said something like this at some point.

Before we look at the labels a comment like this has, let's address what is happening for the child. They're working hard on this project, and after giving it their all, they are looking for excitement and validation. Instead of the father showing excitement, they are met immediately with sarcasm. When we shoot down their enthusiasm with sarcasm, they turn on a negative filter in their mind. Instead of looking for their positives, this filter looks for evidence of where they fall short. When our children are already in a vulnerable spot, sarcasm is not funny; it is destructive.

Each time your child turns on their negative filter, it gets stronger and more present in their life. This filter gets more proficient at extracting negative labels from your words and others around them. It does not take long for labels such as slow, not good enough, not smart enough, and being less than others to take hold of your child. If they start seeing this as who they are, they start acting this way, reinforcing these labels. The hard part is it takes far fewer experiences with negative labels to influence their sense of self than positive and realistic labels.

The vicious cycle of negative labels leading to undesired behavior to reinforce these labels takes a toll on your child. Their identity begins to revolve around these negative labels, and their actions follow along. In time, the perceptions you have of your children can change as you start seeing the behavior you don't want, reinforcing the cycle even more.

It would help if you were mindful of your perceptions and how you express them to your children. Your feedback needs to be positive and realistic to help your child develop a healthy sense of self. However, there are times that your child is going to misbehave, and it needs to be addressed. Let's look at what this situation looks like when focusing on your perceptions.

### Separating Your Child from Their Behavior

As you address your children's misbehavior, you need to

make a strong effort to separate their behavior from their character. When your child does something you disapprove of, ask yourself if you are upset at who your child is or what they have done. The answer is critical because who your child is and what they have done are two very different things, and you need to be sure which one you are addressing.

When you look at the who, this reflects their character, personality, and unique blend of characteristics and traits. Looking at the what is focusing on only their behavior. If you let yourself get out of control, which will be influenced by your perception and interpretation of what is happening, you will father from frustration and anger. The more upset you are, the more likely you will go after who they are, rather than what they have done.

Perhaps an example could help here. Suppose your child has broken a cherished possession that was given to you by someone who means a lot to you. You have told your child numerous times not to touch or play with it. One day you walk into the room to find your child trying hard to use tape and put this item back together so you wouldn't know it was broken. How would you address this situation? What would you say? How would you say it?

If you get worked up enough, chances are you'll have thoughts in your head that sound like, "how in the world could you do that? I have told you over and over not to touch that, and now it's broken because you can't listen or ever do what you are told! You're grounded forever!" Powerful words with lots of negative labels, right? Unfortunately, it's not uncommon when feeling this heated to actually say what you were thinking rather than holding it in. We let our emotions get the best of us, and our perception gets distorted by this emotional reaction.

When we are angry and upset, we unconsciously look for justification for that anger and spread the blame around. Now, most fathers will not go after their children attempting to attack their character. In these moments, we feel like we are trying to correct their behavior, and raising our voice will get that point across. If we say words like the ones above, how harmful or helpful will they be? How might your child take that comment?

Build up your child's self-worth by separating their behavior from their character. Even in a moment like this, you can find a way to include positive and realistic labels. You can use a comment such as, "this is not a good situation, and I am frustrated that I was not listened to. However, I appreciate you trying to solve the problem, and I think you can use those problem-solving skills to keep this from happening in the future." How different is that comment? What will your child think and feel about themselves when you respond in that way?

You can help your child foster healthy and realistic labels that create a strong and positive self-image of themselves. You need to separate their character from their behavior and address the appropriate one. You do not need to over-inflate your child's ego with over-the-top and general praise. Help them form a powerful perception of themselves and who you are as their father rather than forcing your perceptions onto them. To do this effectively, you need to look at how you perceive yourself as a father.

## Your Perception of Yourself

The perception you have of yourself as a father looks at the capabilities your see in yourself, whether or not you feel you measure up to what you think you should be, and the different labels your give yourself. You need to get to know the perceptions you have of yourself for the same reason you need to be concerned with the perceptions your children have of themselves. Just as a child acts in a certain way based on the labels they give themselves, you will do the same thing as a father.

For example, I have worked with many incarcerated fathers who have the perception they are the worst fathers in the world and there is nothing they can do to change this. They are locked up, have lost the ability to be with their children, and feel they have completely failed.

When asked what they are doing to foster and maintain the relationships they have with their children, a typical response was little to nothing. When asked why, they responded that they are the worst father. Their perceptions of being the worst father led them to act this way. As they started to change their behavior and reach out to their children, many were shocked to see how their children saw them and how desperate they were to have their father in their life.

How do you see yourself as a father? Do you find yourself putting either a good or bad label on yourself? It is amazing how we start to ignore the good things we do once we put ourselves in the bad column. Every father who tries will do some awesome stuff while also making some not so good calls. Connecting with the perception you have of yourself allows you to remain realistic even when you've made some mistakes. Remember, perception acts like filters, and there are several you can use on yourself as a father.

### Fatherhood Filters

Let me provide a personal example of a situation that did not go how I wanted to introduce the different filters you might have. My son and I were playing cars in his room, crashing and zooming all over the place. At one point in our energetic play, his vehicle left the floor and flew right into my eye. Let me tell you that did not feel awesome! Out of pure reaction, I yelled, "what are you doing?!?" I ripped the toy from his hand, put it in a box, and angrily walked out of the room. That was how the situation went; let's see how different fatherhood filters could impact my view of myself as a father in this event.

*The Negative Filter.* Does this situation seem familiar to you? Have you ever had a fatherhood moment that did not go the way you wanted? If you have a negative filter on, you will know by the way you think. I'll use myself and the example above to illustrate this.

If I were using a negative filter after walking out of the room, I might be standing in the hall thinking, "man, I just yelled at my son and took his toy away, and he is in there crying his guts out. I must be the worst father ever! I lost it over an accident!"

Do you ever have thoughts like that? How do they influence your perception of yourself as a father? Do you find that when you start talking to yourself like this, your behavior follows along? Does your motivation to try harder and be a better father crumble after giving yourself a beating like that? Negative filters are powerful, but not in a way that helps us out.

*The Prideful Filter.* This filter is where we think we did what was best, and there is no evidence to the contrary. Part of why there is no evidence is that we blame the challenging situation and our negative reactions onto someone else to protect the fragile image we have of ourselves. How do you think that will impact the relationship you have with your child if you use this one frequently?

I'll put on a prideful filter here and see what the car situation would look like with it on. My thoughts may sound like, "I may have had to raise my voice, but he deserved it; he hit me in the eye with a car! If he had followed the rules like he should have been, then I wouldn't have had been hit in the eye or had to yell and take the toy."

This thought process has a lot of finger-pointing to justify our reactions. If this particular line of reasoning struck a chord with you or seems familiar, that may indicate you are using the prideful filter. How would using this filter consistently impact who you grow into as a father? How will it help you reach your goals as a dad? What might be the long-term impacts of using this filter on you, your child, and your relationship?

*The Realistic Filter.* Using this filter means we are looking at the situation to assess what happened realistically. This filter, in the context of the example above, might sound like, "wow, I was caught off guard by the car accidentally hitting my eye that my voice got out of hand, and I took the toy before I could even process what was happening." How different does that sound compared to the Negative and Prideful Filters?

The lack of judgment or assigning blame is absent in this filter. Instead, it helps us to see what occurred and provide a reasonable explanation for the response. This filter does not label us a bad father or blame others; it merely looks at what happened is what happened and nothing else. What would be the benefits of this filter? How does it impact the way you feel about yourself as a father? What would be the benefits for your children?

*The Empowered Filter.* A game-changing filter I want to introduce you to is the Empowered Filter. It's similar to the realistic filter, though it adds some extra components that help you go to the next level. This filter makes sure to add in self-compassion and contemplating what the next steps to take are. Self-compassion is being able to forgive ourselves, see that we are human, and still be a positive, valuable father to our children. This allows us to avoid the shame of the negative filter and the blame of the prideful filter.

Are you wondering what this filter would sound like from the example above? Well, let's find out! "Wow, I was so focused on playing that I did not expect a car to hit my eye! I did react to it by letting my volume rise and swiftly taking the toy before I could even process what happened. It does make sense if I was caught off guard that I would do that, though now I have to figure out what to do about it since my son is in there crying. I need to approach him and let him know I'm sorry I raised my voice and overreacted. I'll let him know I want to go back to the fun we were having, but let's keep the cars on the ground!"

Does that seem like a lot going on? If you answered yes, you are correct; a lot is going on in this statement. It doesn't even compare to the negative or prideful filters! When we use a negative or prideful filter, we take minimal details and run them over and over. We are not looking at the whole situation; instead, we make interpretations from the distorted perceptions the filters provide.

Using the Realistic or Empowered Filters do take more time and energy on your part. I can tell your right now, though, that the effort will be worth it because you will have fewer messes to clean up from the damage of the Negative or Prideful Filters. Remember, your perceptions influence your interpretations, which dictates your behavior. Make sure if you are going to respond to a situation, you have taken the effort to know what is truly going on!

## Growth and Fixed Mindsets

As a father, you need to address a powerful belief related to your perception of yourself. This belief centers on whether you can be flexible and change as needed or feel you are already who you will be and there is nothing that can be done.

These views will have a direct impact on the way you see yourself and behave as a father. If you believe you are who you are already, that is called a fixed mindset. Operating from this mindset sets your beliefs in stone and convinces you that you have the tools you need for fatherhood already in your belt. There is no need to teach a dog new tricks.

For a while, we might get by with this mindset, especially if our children are younger. However, as they grow and develop, it will become apparent, especially to others, that there is a need on our part to change. The fixed mindset makes us believe that others need to change or that our children should behave better. If they would follow our rules, then there would be no problem. Unfortunately, that is not the case, and the issue will be on us.

The more rigid we are in our beliefs, the more we set ourselves up for pain and struggle. Since we will not be open to new ideas, everything and everyone becomes an opponent, locking this mindset even more. This is much more intense than the Negative or Prideful Filters, and it will change the way you perceive your children. Do not let the fixed mindset destroy your relationship with your child; try something different!

Letting go of the fixed mindset will allow us to move into the growth mindset. From this mindset, we do not see ourselves as being set in stone or that we have to operate from one set of beliefs. It helps us understand that there will be times we need to challenge our views before we can father in a situation appropriately. It challenges us to grow and adapt as our children develop. The growth mindset brings some much-needed flexibility to our fathering.

Taking the path of fatherhood puts you on a fantastic journey that will look different for each dad and child. Having a growth mindset rather than fixed allows you to navigate your unique journey more creatively and powerfully. This book and the concept of an Empowered Father is built on the growth mindset. There will always be a need to look at where you are, where you've come from, and what changes are needed to conquer the next part of your journey.

So, how do these two mindsets connect to our perceptions of us as fathers? Let's use one of the biggest challenges we'll face as an example: adolescence. When our children become teenagers, they will be trying to figure out who they are, what they believe, their values, and what they want from life. For some, parental authority can be seen as a barrier to this internal drive to discover their own path.

For fathers with a fixed mindset, these are the years they either buckle down into their views even more or start to see the consequences of their rigidity. A fixed mindset gets in the way of us being able to perceive our abilities as fathers objectively. We believe we are doing the right things and that our children are the ones who are wrong. This biases our perception of our child, just as we discussed earlier in this chapter.

Unfortunately, when we cannot realistically view ourselves and how we contribute to the troubles in our relationship with our children, we will continue to create more of what we do not want. In our child's minds, their perception that we are just heartless authority that wants to take their freedom and individuality away is validated. In our minds, our child's behavior shows us repeatedly that they are at fault, and we are doing the right thing by standing our ground. The fear is that relenting means we lose control and power in the situation. The problem is by not adapting, we have already lost it.

From the growth mindset, we see ourselves constantly evolving as fathers. Adolescence can still be seen as a tough time as our children will continue to fight for their freedoms and find out who they are. Having a growth mindset provides the flexibility necessary to help our children navigate this new time in their lives. At the same time, we also maintain a healthy and realistic perception of our child.

From this flexibility, our perceptions of us as fathers and our children and their behavior are more realistic. Empowered Fathers do not see flexibility as losing power and control to our children; rather, it is a way to yield it more appropriately by providing our children with opportunities to learn about responsibility. We can adapt to the changes in the relationship we have with our child as they develop, which only deepens our connection levels.

Having a fixed mindset is like putting a diagnosis on ourselves and believing things are the way they are, and there is nothing that can be done about it. The growth mindset allows us to assess where we are to help make any necessary course corrections. No fatherhood journey is the same, and it will come with a ton of unpredictability. Do yourself a favor and recognize there is room for growth and change on your part.

As an Empowered Father, seek to form a realistic perception of yourself and your children. Continually seek alternative explanations for the behavior you see rather than jumping to conclusions. When necessary, take accountability for your contributions to negative cycles in your relationship rather than blaming them. Help coach your children on the power of taking accountability as well. Challenge your perceptions when necessary, whether it is about one of your children or yourself. Recognize that growth and flexibility are not obstacles but rather tools that can help you overcome obstacles on your journey.

## Final Thoughts

Perceptions can be a tricky topic to cover. Each of us has our own ways of perceiving the world. We build our view of reality based on our perceptions. Our behavior and responses will be based on the interpretations we make from our perceptions. That is quite an abstract concept, but it has a direct impact on how we father.

Having an open mind allows us to realize that the way we perceive and interpret what is happening is only one possibility. Being open means that we will take the time to develop alternate views, give our children a chance to explain what happened, and knowing that our perceptions and interpretations could be wrong. Remember that one dad who turned it into a game of detective? That's precisely what we are going for!

Perception has incredible power over us. The way we view ourselves as dads impacts the way we father. A realistic perception means that we know we will make mistakes, may need to apologize, will do incredible things, and that no matter what, we will care for our children. This will allow us to grow and adapt as we move through this amazing journey.

A negative perception of ourselves leads to shaming every wrong we do, sometimes avoiding interaction because of our fear of messing up or labeling ourselves as a failure. When we use these labels and believe them, we lock ourselves within their limits. We start to think that no matter what we do, we will run into failure. Keep in mind, as fathers, we will act the way we believe we are, so be careful with those labels!

Our behavior influences this same process within our children. They begin to form the picture they have of themselves based on how others react and respond to them. As their father, our reactions and behavior carry a ton of weight. They also begin to act the way they believe they are. This has enormous implications for their levels of self-worth and self-esteem in addition to impacting their future relationships.

The more information we allow in to influence our perception, the closer to reality it will be. However, the more rigid we are, the less we will see reality. This type of closed-mindedness will have detrimental consequences and potentially cause irreparable damage to our relationships with our children. Take the time to explore alternate explanations and try new things as a father because there is always room for growth!

# | 8 |

# The Power of Modeling

This seems like an excellent place to review what we have covered in our journey so far. We have looked into what we value, where our morals lie, and our beliefs and goals. We've explored emotions and the importance they have for the health of ourselves and our children. You have examined your needs around control and the perceptions you have and how they influence how you father. This chapter aims to help take these constructs to the next level by looking at how they show through our behavior.

There is a reason we need to break down these ideas and how they influence our behavior. The truth is our behavior is what others around us see, and what it shows them is a window into our character. The more aligned we are with these core constructs, the more our behavior will reflect it. Your behavior will either give you away or show your integrity; it can't lie or conceal your true character. Our behavior is one of the most powerful tools we have as fathers.

The term researches use for the power of our behavior to teach our children is modeling. Luckily, the modeling we are talking about does not involve a catwalk in Paris or an intense photoshoot. As a father, you are already a model. You provide an example to your children of how people behave and interact through your behavior. We can model behavior either intentionally or unintentionally. Your behavior is always on display; it is up to you to be mindful of what you do because your children's eyes are incredibly perceptive and rarely miss anything!

### Intentional and Unintentional Modeling

You might be wondering what intentionally or unintentionally modeling means. Quite simply, we are always behaving, which means we are always exhibiting some example for our children to learn from. Intentional modeling is when we know our children are watching, so we demonstrate behavior that aligns with our core selves. We bring our A-game and model not lying, being courteous to others, cleaning up after ourselves, doing dishes, being respectful and kind to our partner, and love by playing with our children. Each of these behaviors are things we would be happy to see them repeat, which they are more likely to do if they see you doing them!

Unintentional modeling is the times we forget we are on stage and behave in a way we do not want our children to see or repeat. Instead of displaying honesty, we might tell a small lie. Rather than demonstrate an appropriate way to handle frustration, we lose our temper and see it on repeat when they do the same thing later. The best parents in the world engage in unintentional modeling because we are all human. To be the most effective with this tool, you need to focus more on your intentional modeling so you can start reducing the amount of unintentional modeling you are doing. I want to take a quick moment to tell you about one of my unintentional modeling stories that has come back to bite me a few times to help make this point.

### To Throw or Not to Throw

I have struggled with anger throughout my life, and while I seem calm all the time to many, not far below the surface lies quite the temper. While I have learned to manage myself, there are times it still wins and gets the best of me. That is one reason I can't play golf with my children around!

However, this story takes place on the driveway working on my truck and not the golf course. I was attempting to repair the brake sensor that had one out under my pedal. My son, who was two-years-old at the time, was hanging out with me. He's a big fan of the truck and being like his dad while working on it, so he was taking a screwdriver to anything he could to fix the truck as well.

While working on this sensor, I kept running into the same problem. I could get the sensor locked in place, but the brake lights would not come on when I pressed down on the pedal. After a few attempts of taking the sensor out and putting it back in, and still no brake lights, my anger started to build. My son was sitting in the front seat, and I'm sure he could see my face was turning the color the brake lights were supposed to be. Knowing he was watching, I took a deep breath and told him, "We just keep trying, buddy." Pretty good intentional modeling on my part, right?

Being true to my statement, I did try again, several times, with the same result. My frustration got the better of me, and I had an adult tantrum and threw the wrench I was using across the yard. Not only did that moment cost me my favorite socket, I turned around to see my son staring straight at me. Trying to play it off like it was no big deal, I shrugged my shoulders and went back to work.

After a while, I did figure it out and solved the problem, and we finished for the day. I did not think anything more of my outburst or that it was a big deal until a week or so later. My son had just gotten a new trainset where the trains connect with magnets and the tracks look like wooden puzzle pieces. He was attempting to put the track together in a way that would look cool but was not feasible with the pieces he had.

I could see him starting to struggle, so I asked if he needed help. He said every two-year-old's favorite word, no, and kept on trying. It impressed me how he was trying to figure it out, and I couldn't help but think of that day in the driveway where we talked about not giving up and keep on trying. I won't lie; I let myself have a small, proud dad moment until that moment was over suddenly.

He grew too frustrated to try again, which led him to pick up the pieces and throw them against the wall. While my jaw dropped in shock, he grabbed another piece and threw that one too. By the time I got over to him, another piece had left the runway and headed to its destination. Not only had I intentionally modeled for my son to keep trying, but I had also unintentionally modeled for him to let his inner quarterback out when he was mad and let it fly!

This behavior, which I wish I could say was gone completely, has resurfaced numerous times when his temper has flared. Each time I see it happen, my mind can't help but go back to that day on the driveway where he saw me throw that wrench. It was this experience that taught me not only the power of intentional modeling but also the influence unintentional modeling has as well.

Our children's brains are like sponges, and each moment they are soaking up what they see around them. As their parent, you are their first teacher in life. You will teach them lessons on what is important, what to tolerate and what not to, how a person should act, and so many other things. You might notice these are similar to your morals, values, and the ability to regulate your emotions. Keep in mind that we are always teaching our children something, and it pays to be an intentional model so there is a higher chance of seeing more of what you want to see rather than the opposite!

Have you had the experience of trying to teach your children about the words please and thank-you, and they don't seem to say it the way you'd like? Yet, you swear out loud only once, and next thing you know, you hear it come out of their young mouths? We do not always get to choose what our children will pick up and use from our behavior; however, you have a better show when you use intentional modeling. Of course, we will not always be intentional, so where does that unintentional behavior come from? Let's find out!

### Why Did You Do That?!?

Has there been a time where your child did something

that wasn't a big deal, yet you went off like a grenade? Doesn't it suck even more when you see your child react in the same way later on? This connects to our previous discussion on values. When our child does something that presses one of our buttons, our behavior is more likely to move from intentional to unintentional as we start to lose control of ourselves in the situation.

It may seem like talking about emotions or analyzing our beliefs is more suited for a therapy office. However, as a father, this is critical for you to do. If you neglect getting to know yourself, you will pay the price later with the behavior you teach your children. There are times that you will have created the negative behavior in your children because they are merely playing back to you what they saw you do. The more unaware you are of what goes on inside you, the more you will show and see these behaviors.

Think back to your childhood. Did you ever hear a parent say something along the lines of "do as I say, not as I do?" How did you react to this statement when you were a child? Have you found yourself using it with your children? It's a statement that we intuitively know is not effective, but we might live by it more than we think, especially if we are using unintentional more than intentional modeling.

Let's examine this "do as I say, not as I do" comment closely. What seems to be its implied message? That's probably obvious, as it means my words are more important, so listen to them. The funny thing is, this comment points out its own hypocrisy. The message we are verbally presenting is different than the one we are showing through our actions.

It's also attempting to control which lesson they will internalize, which is a wrong move.

Recall with control that when we try wrestling it away from our child, they are likely to do the opposite of what we want. Because of this, our child ignores the "do as I say" part and choose to follow what we do instead. This gives them a sense of control in the situation. Also, children are excellent imitators. They learn to navigate their world by what they see more than what they hear. That is where we get into trouble if we are not aware of our behavior.

While you may not like this quote, you could be living by it more than you realize. Perhaps when your children are upset and yelling at one another, you yell out, "quit yelling at your brother!" We are attempting to stop the yelling in the house by modeling that we can solve conflict through yelling. Do as I say - stop yelling, not as I do - yelling to get you to stop. In this instance, you just lived by that quote.

The truth is all of us at some point have used some variation of the "do as I say, not as I do" comment. We are human, and there will be times that we use this comment as a formula for our behavior. The more aware you become of who you are, the less likely you will use this to guide your behavior.

Unintentional modeling of negative behavior comes from a disconnect between knowing and living our morals, values, beliefs, and goals. It comes from mismanaged emotions, not appropriately meeting our need for control, and having distorted perceptions. The more we run on auto-pilot, the less we know about these powerful inner parts of ourselves. Our negative behavior comes when we are not aligned with these core constructs, and this internal conflict comes out to play ball on the relational field our children share with us.

Our behavior is a window into our character. The more aware we are of what goes on inside us, the more transparent we will be through our behavior. Modeling ties these different constructs' power into one package that either helps build our children or pulls them down. If we believe there are better ways than yelling to solve an interpersonal conflict, we will show it through how we treat them.

Your behavior can be a powerful model for your children when your values, morals, beliefs, goals, emotions, needs for control, and perceptions have a synergistic flow. They can work as one rather than being competing forces. The more you get yourself to align within, the more your behavior will reflect that.

Modeling is one of the most powerful tools you have as a father when working with your children. That is why you need to try as hard as you can each day to provide examples of what you would like to see rather than what you do not. While it is a powerful tool, modeling is also tricky to use correctly because it is always in use, even when we do not want it to be!

There are many distractions in life, making it difficult for us to remember that we are always modeling. Our children may be more aware of our behavior than we are! This is a good thing when we unintentionally model good things to our children, which happens when we are still aligned with our core constructs. Here's a quick story to illustrate.

A father in one of my classes bragged about a weekend at the pond with his son when he noticed the child picking up garbage and throwing it away. He asked his son where he learned this, and he pointed at his dad. The last time they were at the park, this man had picked up several empty cans near a group of baby ducks. While not thinking about it, he had modeled to his son to take care of the environment, something of high value to this father. When we are aligned within, we can use modeling to our advantage, even when we do not consciously think about it.

When our children are young, they want to find their place in a world that seems too big for them. To do this, they turn to those who mean the most to them, their parents. We give them ideas and tools for coping with the world they live in by the things we do. Messages are always being sent through our behavior. Children are often the best mirror in the house. If you want a peek at what you are like, just watch your child!

Take a moment to think about a couple of questions. As you think about the answers you come up with, consider how they impact your effectiveness as a father. As always, if you need to make a change, get a plan together to make it happen. Now, to the questions. What am I intentionally modeling well and will keep doing? What am I unintentionally modeling that I would like to change? Remember, the more aware you are of what you are doing, the more you will demonstrate behavior that leads to outcomes that create harmony rather than tension in our homes!

### Modeling for Life

One of the crucial things about modeling is that it is a

critical tool for teaching our children how to navigate their world. Our children are always watching how we interact with others, solve problems, handle emotions, and so much more. Our children's brains absorb our behaviors to make a blueprint of how they will be. As a father, we need to grow in our intentionality of how we interact with them and others to help make this work in everyone's favor. You have the responsibility as a father to help your children learn how to navigate their world.

Your children will also learn from you how to interact with others. When they see you having a conflict with their mother or another adult, they begin learning about conflict resolution or lack thereof. If you turn to sarcasm, anger, yelling, or forcing your way through to get what you want to get the victory no matter the cost, chances are they will try to do the same. Think about when you and your child are in a power struggle. What behaviors do they have that are similar to yours?

Relationships are a complicated part of life. Your children will learn many of the skills they take into their relationships based on what they have observed us do with them and others. Of course, school, friends, and other influences will come into play throughout their lives, but you are their first and primary teacher.

Being a father, you will teach your sons how to act like a man from your actions more than your words. You will teach him how to interact with others and treat women. If you don't know your inner-views and beliefs, you need to get connected with them quickly! For your daughter, you will teach her how other men in her life should treat her. Based on your example, what do you think she is learning? Is there room for change?

The way you treat your children and how they observe you treat others provides a blueprint for them on how to act in their relationships. This has a significant impact on their future relationships and the way they will parent one day. You can prepare your children for life in a more powerful way than words; you can show them!

## Final Thoughts

Modeling is the culmination of the topics we have discussed in this book so far. It is the outward way you teach your children about your values and beliefs. They will learn about how you see and feel about them from the way you treat them. When it comes to emotions and their ability to regulate them, they will turn to you as an example. Your behavior shows a lot more of the true you than your words, so what are you showing your children?

One of the main reasons we have discussed the particular topics in this book is because of modeling. The more you know yourself in a deeper way, including what you believe and stand for and where your strengths and challenges lie, the more your behavior will align with your core self. If you do not know where you stand or what you believe, what will your behavior teach your children?

Remember that modeling is always happening, whether we are aware of it or not. I thought I had modeled for my son to persevere and not give up until you find a viable solution.

While I did manage to start that lesson, I also unintentionally modeled for him what to do when you get angry, and that was throw something. Make modeling work in your favor by being more intentional.

If you get mad at your child's misbehavior often, it would be prudent to look at yourself first and see if you are mad because they are acting like you. Is it fair to punish your child if they act like you from the example you gave them? It's our responsibility to be aware of what we are teaching our children through our actions and words. If there are things that need to change, be the one to start that change. Model for your children what you want to see them do. Empowered Fathers admit their shortcomings and take steps to correct them. That is a powerful lesson to model to your children and is a gift that will keep on giving throughout their lives!

# | 9 |

# Let's Talk about Communication

Communication is essential for human connection. We can never not communicate. Even if we give the silent treatment, we are still communicating something because communication is more than words. While every relationship depends on it, communication is not an easy process. That process takes on new complexity when you look at the father-child relationship.

The way you communicate with your children has far-reaching effects on both your child's and your life. The messages you communicate and how you do it directly links with the relational bank account. It can help determine whether you are making a withdrawal or a deposit. Let's break down some communication principles to help determine what is useful and what is not.

**Message Sent**

Our world has grown to depend on technology for communication more than any other generation. It is amazing that something can happen on the other side of the world, and in moments it is popping up on our phones. We are more globally connected than we have ever been, and yet, at home, it can seem like we are more disconnected than we have ever been.

The use of text messaging and email has seemingly over-simplified the process in some ways. We input a message, watch the little circle as it sends, and then get a confirmation when it arrives at the other end. After a few moments, or what can sometimes seem like forever, we receive a reply. From here, we send another message, and on and on it goes. Seems easy enough, right?

Unfortunately, there is a lot more going on when we communicate face-to-face with someone. When we write a text or email, there is some security because we can look at the message, edit it, put in some emojis or gifs, or delete it entirely and start over before we send it. When we are physical with a person, that goes out of the window, and the dynamics change.

There is more to communicating than just a string of words. Take the statement, "it's good to be home." Perhaps you know there is going to be a party when you get home, so when you walk through the door, you energetically exclaim, "it's good to be home!" Or, maybe it has been a long and stressful day, and as soon as you open the door, you are met with screams, toppled over furniture, and a lovely piece of artwork your 2-year-old has added to the wall. Your mumbled, "it's good to be home," replaces energy and enthusiasm with sarcasm and defeat. It is not just the words we use; it is the other ways we express that matter.

Your face-to-face communication comes with a lot of other clues to help send your real message. You provide many nonverbal cues, such as your posture, where your eyes are looking, what you do with your hands, and where you stand in proximity to the other person. We process a lot of these cues unconsciously, and we lean towards body language and other cues rather than words to extract the message.

Our children are learning to communicate, and we are one of their primary teachers. As they communicate with us, their brain's different parts specialized for communication are formed and strengthened. The words we use and the way we say them help these areas of their brains develop. Getting in touch with the way we communicate helps make sure we are 1) sending the right message and 2) sending it the way we want it to be received.

This process gets even more complicated by the way you and your child unconsciously influence one another. For example, if your child sees your body language as tense and closed, they may grow tense and closed in response. This changes the way we see them at that moment and how we deliver our message. Let's use an example to demonstrate this process.

Suppose your child has broken a toy that you recently purchased for them, even though money was tight and it was a splurge you were not sure you could make. If they are carrying the toy and its pieces to you in both hands so they can tell you what happened, your brain is already running through and trying to figure out the situation. If your emotions get the best of you and you react, you may focus on the broken toy and your frustration that comes with it rather than your heartbroken child.

These emotional reactions lead you to tense up, flare out your chest, cross your arms, and get steam blowing out of your ears like a Saturday morning cartoon character. Your intense reactions and body language have impacted your child before you have even said a single word. They are already beginning to predict what will happen just based on what they see from you. Again, no words have even been said yet, and our communication is already off and running.

Some children may cower and pull inside, no longer wanting to say anything as they grow fearful of you. That is a massive withdrawal from the relational bank account. Some children match your intensity and begin to yell and fight back. Still, this a significant withdrawal from the relational bank account. Others may simply avoid you and try to run and hide. This is also a withdrawal from the relational bank account and does not foster trust. Now that we know we can influence each other through body language, let's look at some general thoughts to make it work to your benefit.

### Body Language

Before we get going on this discussion, I just want to bring up the point again that over 70% of communication is nonverbal. Let that sink in for just a second to help recognize how important your body language is with your child. The way you hold and use your body in conversation makes or breaks a situation with your child. You may think you know what your body is saying, but the reality is many of us are un-aware. The way you use your body will help establish safety and trust for your child or the opposite. Body language is that powerful!

Body language establishes safety and trust when it aligns with the words you are saying. Having a look of concern when asking your child if they are okay after falling off their bike eases their fear that we will be mad at them. If you have a scowl on your face and biting your lip to mask that you are mad they scratched the bike in the crash, your words will not have the same impact. Your body language can create a sense of fear in your child over the situation.

Body language is another reason we addressed emotions in a previous chapter. Our emotions have a direct impact on the body language we show. In fact, our body language is the outward way we will show our emotions to others. If we hold something in and do not address those emotions, it will sneak out in our body language. To help keep your body language and verbal message aligned, manage your emotions. Make the relationship between your emotions and body language work in your favor.

The way we hold our bodies with our posture communicates to the other person our level of interest in the interaction. We can fold our arms and lean back, which communicates we are closed to the conversation and want distance. We might avoid giving adequate eye contact or stare too long, which will make the other person uncomfortable. When we have not managed our emotions, we magnify it in our body language and make it more intense.

Body language gives off many clues, especially if we are

not interested in the conversation. Any time that we look at our watches, pull out a phone, refuse to nod our head, cross our arms, or clench our hands into fists communicates disinterest. The more you know your emotional state, the more you will control your body language.

What if we are upset and want to come off more domineering? Actively choosing to be upset presents different body language. We enlarge our posture like a rooster, pushing out our chest to give the illusion that we are bigger than we are. We clench our fists, push out our chest, flex our arms, tighten our jaws, and angle our posture towards the person to minimize space. Our eyes are locked on them to communicate our anger. If you do not learn to manage your emotions, especially anger, you will go into a situation with your child just like this. How productive will that be for you and your child?

How do we make body language work in our favor? What do we need to do to communicate we are interested and present? A big part is merely relaxing your body. Let your arms hang down a bit rather than trying to cross them or your hands. This can be tough because men like to cross their arms in general. If you feel the need to cross your arms, try to make it a loose and relaxed grip rather than tight to avoid coming off as closed. Regular eye contact and head nodding show we are present and listening. When we genuinely want to listen, our body language will follow along.

One way to help illustrate positive body language is for you to identify a meaningful example. Think of someone you know that you feel the most open with because of security and trust levels. Focus on their body language for a moment rather than their words. How do they convey to you they are open and can be trusted? What lets you know they care? What can you learn about how they use their body when communicating that you can apply to your relationship with your child?

It is important to know your body language to be more proactive rather than reactive in your communication. Remember, the body language you have influences your child and vice versa. If you do not think of this process, your conversation could be doomed before any words are said. It takes a lot of effort to keep your body calm, especially if you feel attacked. Your body language creates an environment of security and trust for your child to help them be more open. Empowered Fathers use this to the relationship's advantage by combining it with how they speak to their children.

### The Way We Speak

The way you voice your message contributes to the way your child receives it. Our tone is made up of the inflections we put in our voice and the volume we use. They interact and influence how our child will interpret our words. Let's start by looking at inflection.

Inflection is the tempo, intensity, and energy you put into your words. Let's use the example "this is the best" to demonstrate this as best as we can in a book. If you were on a roller coaster having the time of your life, you might yell out, "this is the best!" as you bank quickly around the turns. Can you imagine the energy and enthusiasm in those words? If we are sarcastic because we have to have dinner with someone we do not like, we might mumble, "this...is...the...best." It is slower with a lack of energy that helps convey the disgust we feel at that moment.

It is tough to discuss inflection in a book without a voice to go with it. It's like trying to decipher a text message. Have you ever gotten a text from someone and you try to guess what they are saying just based on grammar and punctuation marks? It's hard to do and messes with our mood, which influences how we interpret the text. Our mood, when in person, also affects the way we say something. The energy and inflection you put into your words will give the person a clue to your mood and emotional state in addition to how much it means to you.

Volume is another tool we use to help convey our message. Any message can change into something else by simply changing the volume. Take the words, "I love you." Say it calmly and with a decent volume, and your child will interpret it that way. Add a deep volume, or make it loud, and it might come off as a threat or sarcasm. Our children sensitive to volume and inflection and use it as a way to gauge where we are. There's a trick to making volume work in your favor. Turn it down so you can tune in and listen!

### Time to Listen!

Sending your message is only one part of communication. Listening is the second and most crucial part of the equation. Learning effective listening skills takes time to master, but the more emphasis you put into practicing them, the more you will see a return on that investment. Often, we say we are listening when we are distracted and not truly attuned to our child and their message. The easiest way to know when you are not listening is to recognize when you are formulating your own responses when your child is still talking.

If you are not tuning in to the messages you are receiving from your child, you miss out on a full understanding. Without a full understanding, you are more likely to jump to conclusions and *react* rather than stay locked in and connected with your child. This leads to withdrawals from your relationship that never needed to happen!

We want others to listen to us and feel deep appreciation when they show they truly understand what we are saying and experiencing. Our children are no different when it comes to wanting to feel this way. They especially want to feel this from you, their father! It is not fair on your part to demand that they listen to you without listening to them. This is where modeling comes in. Model listening, and you will see it in return. Don't listen and expect to see the same thing. The choice is yours!

Not listening communicates a lack of interest on your part to your child. You might see it as you are not interested in the topic; however, your child will internalize it that you are not interested in them. Our children test that we will be there and listen to them with big topics through simple conversations about things that may not interest us. Choosing to listen or not impacts the trust and security in your relationship.

We are not showing our child respect when we choose not to listen to them. Feeling respect is often a valued feeling for people. When we do not model respect to our children through listening, is it fair to expect them to listen to us? After all, they are just doing what we taught them!

If there are going to be barriers to you being able to listen fully, let them know. You can always say, "I can tell what you want to talk about is big to you, and I want to hear you, let me get this phone call out of the way so that it won't distract me from listening. Let's get back together in 10 minutes." Be genuine, let them know you truly want to hear what they have to say, and make sure you get back together. You influence the expectations they have of you based on experience. If you come back and listen, they know you will be there when they need you most. If you don't, then they will find someone else to talk with. Manage yourself in the times it is hard to listen because they will happen.

What gets in the way of listening and makes it hard to do? First off, let's just put it out there; listening is tough to do. It is hard to hold our attention to what is going on while piecing together all the information. That also includes distractions like a cell phone vibrating or your team playing on the TV in the playoffs. There are many distractions out there, and they have trained us to have a short attention span. This is in complete contrast to listening, which is a slow and time-consuming process. So, is it worth the effort?

Taking the time to listen to our children to understand creates collaboration and builds our children's character. Instead of their inner voice saying, "I'm not interesting or worth it to my father," it says, "I am worth it to my father because I have worth." When that happens, what do you think happens to the relational bank account? The balance goes through the roof! Also, our example will show them how to listen and the importance of it.

Now, how do we do this listening thing? I want you to think of the person you can talk to again. What do they do that makes you feel like you can talk to them? Do they interrupt you every three seconds or tell you what to do without hearing the full story? Are they texting while you talk? Do their comments have nothing to do with what you are saying? Of course not! Why would we talk to someone who acts that way?

Now, put yourself in your child's shoes. If you respond quickly with your interpretation without letting them speak or just show disinterest in what they have to say, what is that doing for your child? Are they going to want to come to you when they have a problem? Do you want your children to feel enough trust and safety with you that they come and talk to you about sex, drugs, or alcohol? Are you listening in a way that is building that safety and trust?

### Listening Like a HERO

All of us could make improvements to the way we listen to our children. There is a continuous learning curve for listening. To help you out with this, let's examine what it takes to listen like a HERO. Empowered Fathers become a HERO in communication when they listen with Humility, Empathy, Respect, and Open-Mindedness. Let's dig into each of these components a little deeper.

## Humility

Humility is vital when it comes to being a great listener to your children. As their father, you have lived longer and have more experience than they do. While the wisdom that comes with this is excellent to have, there are times it gets in the way of you listening. You may try to fill in the gaps of their message with your experience. This usually stops one from listening and moves you into a speaker role, or most likely, a lecturer. This move might be well-intended, as you want to keep your child from some of the painful experiences you had. I'm cautioning and encouraging you to overcome this urge!

If you want to truly be present with your child when communicating, having humility will help you overcome that urge. It will say a lot about you as a father when you set aside your ego, views, and desire to say what is on your mind so you can be fully present with your child. You have great things to say, but it is all about timing.

When we are the listener, our most important task is to listen to comprehend and understand. Be humble and set aside what you want to say for now so you can listen to your child. Your words will have more power when you time them right and your child feels heard. You might be surprised how your child responds to you and how much the relational bank account builds up. If you want your child to feel secure and trust you enough to come to you with the hard stuff, this is how you do it!

## Empathy

To make your listening go to the next level, you need to be able to put yourself in the shoes of your child. That is where empathy comes into play. Empathy allows you to get out of your head and experiences by putting yourself in your child's experience. Empathy automatically changes the perspective you have of your child. You will not turn to harsh lectures or "do this" suggestions. Instead, you will look for a deeper understanding of your child.

Empathy is not an easy skill to learn, and I must warn you that it does not come naturally for every man. If you have grown up believing that males push their emotions down or steer clear of them, this will be a different experience for you. To help out, think back again to the person you go to when you need to talk to someone. How do they show you empathy? What do they do that lets you know they are experiencing as close as possible to what you are?

Keep in mind that empathy is not sympathy; it is much deeper than that. Sympathy is feeling sorry for someone, whereas empathy is attempting to join them in their experience to understand what they are going through. It's taking the time to reach a deeper connection with the other person as you truly immerse yourself in their world. You need to do that for your children if you want them to feel secure and that they can trust you. It might require you to get out of your comfort zone, but by now, that should be par for the course with being an Empowered Father!

## Respect

I have yet to work with a father who did not want their children's respect and vice versa. However, that does not mean that everyone goes about it the same way. I have worked with those who believe they have every right to demand their child's respect and then don't understand why it isn't there as they use their authority. Fear does not breed respect; it generates more fear and resistance.

Other dads understand that they are more likely to see it back when treating their children with respect. This is a situation where the rule of what comes around, goes around comes into play. The way you treat your children is often what you will receive back. If you model respect to your children, you are more likely to be treated with respect.

Taking the time to focus on your children and providing your undivided attention while listening is a sign of respect. They know that you are connecting with them, and each word they are allowed to say strengthens that connection. When you respect your child, they will be more open with you. This does not mean that you will agree with everything they say and let it slide. Instead, it means you give them a chance to tell their story, which provides you with more information to respond appropriately. Demonstrate respect now, and you will see it returned to you.

## Open-Mindedness

Being open-minded ties all the other components of listening like a HERO together. Even though we have talked about them separately, they work synergistically and won't work without the other parts. Without an open-mind, listening in this way will be nearly impossible as it will not show respect or empathy, and humility will go out the window.

Having an open mind does not mean you will stray from your values or the expectations you have set up in the home. Your child also doesn't get to do or say whatever they want to, either. Rather, being open-minded means that you are good with the idea of your child having a chance to speak. This allows you to consider what they say before you respond. It keeps you from becoming rigid in your control, perceptions, and reactions. Unfortunately, if you let that happen, you will miss out on the bigger picture of strengthening the connection you have with your children!

As your child tells their side of the story, be open to what they tell you. When you set your ego aside and show your child respect by listening to them, it is surprising how the picture changes. There might be information you didn't know that changes the way you need to respond. If you're not open to different possibilities or what your child says, your listening and relationship with your child will crumble.

Now that you have a better grasp on what it means to listen like a HERO, take a moment to reflect on some questions. When it comes to listening like a HERO, where do you feel you are doing well? What areas would others say you are doing well with? Which one might be harder for you, and why? If there is an area of being a HERO that is difficult for you, it might be worth starting here. To help you out even further, let's look at a few listening skills and tips that can help change the game!

## Listening Skills and Tips

While listening is an art, there are skills you can learn to help give you an advantage. These skills require practice because you can't master them from reading them in a book. It is crucial to try them out in all your relationships, not just the ones with your children. They will be most effective when they become part of you, and that happens by using them in all your relationships. If there is a skill that is brand new to you, be patient and realistic. Learn from the times it goes well and the times that it does not; either way, just know there will always be something to learn!

### Clear Picture Questions

If you want to increase your understanding of what your child is saying, Clear Picture Questions are what you need! As your child speaks, you put together a picture in your head about what they are saying and how they feel, think, and react. Clear Picture Questions will help fill in the missing puzzle pieces in your picture. Use these questions to help keep you from filling in the missing details with your own guesses, views, assumptions, and opinions. A Clear Picture Question sounds something like:

*"You said you last remember your soccer ball in your bag, but when you just looked, it was not there, and you don't know where the ball is. I may have missed a detail. When you last knew the ball*

*was in the bag, was that while you were at practice or somewhere else?"*

The great things about these questions are they show you are listening and trying to understand while also getting your child thinking about what is going on in a new way. Children are like us and can get fixated on small details and lose sight of the bigger picture. Clear Picture Questions help clarify for you what is going on while reducing fixation and widening their views. This is a win-win situation if you make sure you ask with genuineness and curiosity rather than sarcasm!

### Paraphrasing

One of the most effective ways to demonstrate you are listening is to paraphrase what you have heard. This does not mean you become a parrot and recite word for word what your child said. Paraphrasing is condensing the message down to its critical points. They do not need to be a long-winded speech, which is counterproductive and will be strange for you and your child. Try to make it as concise as possible, using only the essential details.

Paraphrasing requires us to mentally keep track of what has been said while simultaneously tuning in to what is currently being said. If we let too many details grow on our mental list, we will lose focus and miss what our child is saying. When you start to feel that you can't hold onto all the information you need to, politely interrupt your child. Saying something along the lines of, "let me see if I understand this correctly" is a helpful way to accomplish this. Doing this opens a door for you to do a quick paraphrase.

An awesome benefit of paraphrasing is that even if you are off a little bit on what they've said, you'll still be in a good spot. If you are wrong and your child says something like, "no, dad, that's not it, it's this," you still win. Your child will clarify what you missed, which still moves you closer to understanding. Hopefully, that takes a bit of stress off on making sure you get it 100% correct because guess what, you won't, and that is okay! To help out with paraphrasing, here are a few examples:

*"It sounds like the start of school has been a little rougher than you were expecting, with some friends no longer acting like they did last year and some harder classes."*

*"You had a fun time on your date, but now you are wondering why he hasn't called you."*

*"Let me see if I am catching what you are saying. This weekend you would rather go to your friend's house to work on your school project than go to your aunt's house."*

*"You are not sure about asking that girl to the dance because she has said no to you before and you do not want to go through that again, even though you like her. Is that right?"*

*"You are not sure why Jimmy wouldn't share his truck and that it's not fair because you shared your airplane."*

Even though these statements have no context to them, can you see how paraphrasing gets the gist of it? Are you able to tell what is going on without any context? It is a powerful tool that can help you out a ton!

A few words of caution. Try not to add judgment or your own take on things in your paraphrase. It might be easy to slip in something like, "I don't see why it's such a big deal that he did not call you back after your date, he isn't that cool of a kid." How different does that sound? What will your child hear if you add in your views? The goal is to build a connection through understanding, and paraphrasing is fantastic for that!

### Empathy

This word should look familiar; it's a big part of listening like a HERO! Empathy is a skill you can use to convey you are there with your child and searching for a deeper understanding and connection than through just words alone. Empathy can come in comments, such as, "Wow, that must have been really hard for you" or "Life just sucks sometimes, doesn't it?" It can also be your arm around their shoulder or a hug when they are hurting emotionally. It takes time and practice while requiring you to set aside any agendas or thoughts you have about the situation. Eliminating judgment and replacing it with empathy is more than worth the effort, and the strong relationship you will build with your child will be proof of that!

### Small Acknowledgements

You can do small things while your child talks to show them you are present and listening. These small acknowledgments include leaning towards your child to narrow the gap to create connection, nodding your head when appropriate, and verbal sounds and statements like "yeah" or "mmhmm." When you listen intently and are genuinely absorbed in what your child is saying, most of these will come naturally. These are different cues to your child that you are processing what they are saying. Do know that if you are doing these just to do them, your child will know you are not being genuine and will probably call you out on it!

### A Few Things to Keep in Mind

You can use these tips to take your relationship with your child to a whole new level as they make exceptional deposits into your account. Reading them in a few paragraphs might give the appearance that they are easy; just know that is not always the case. They take time to master, especially if they are a brand-new approach for you. We need to cover a couple of things that might get in the way of you feeling like you can do it or that they are worth it.

*Frustration.* Let's face it; sometimes, communicating with your child is just plain frustrating. When we are frustrated, it is easy for us to get overly focused on what has happened. The more frustrated we get and allow it to control us, the more ineffective we will communicate. We will turn to lecture rather than listening, conclusions over clarity, and disengagement instead of engagement.

Managing our frustration is part of regulating our emotions. Hopefully, at this point, you have gotten to know your emotional self more thoroughly, including where your strengths and limitations lie. This will allow you to take proactive steps to help you better regulate your frustration so you can continue to listen. Doing this will keep you from *re-*

*acting*, which leads to making a bigger problem and massive withdrawals from your relational bank account.

You also need to know what it feels like during the times you are not going to hold yourself together. When you reach this point, you need to be the bigger person and pause the conversation to take a break and resume it later when you can be more effective. There is nothing wrong with saying, "I do want to hear what you have to say, but right now I'm upset and won't be able to give you the attention needed, so let's take a pause and come back to this."

Taking a break will allow you to relax and drop your frustration levels. This will increase your ability to listen and make good judgment calls when you come back together. More importantly, it models for your child how to manage their own emotions, especially when interacting with others. We want to teach them that problems are better resolved or dealt with then there is dialogue and progress rather than *reaction* and conflict. I encourage you to give it a try to prevent the danger of pushing through when highly frustrated and agitated. This will help build trust and security, and your child will want to come to you in the future!

**Time.** Our world is always moving, and it seems more people are saying they do not have enough time to do what they want or need to do. It is true, there are a lot of things pressing for our time, and as you've read this chapter, you might have thought it's not realistic to take the time needed to listen to your child. However, we need to think of what that is actually saying. Do you really not have the time, or are you just unwilling to make the time? Are you just wanting things to stay the same? If you genuinely want to build a strong and enduring relationship with your child, believe that your child is worth it and find the time!

*Patience.* Is there anything that tests our patience more than being a father? Have you ever been in a situation where your child is taking forever to tell a 30-second story? Even though it can be hard to remain focused, you need to have the patience to stay in the listener role. If you do not allow your child the chance to speak, chances are you will turn on lecturer mode and do the speaking for them. We've already talked about how that is not a helpful thing to do! Be patient with your child, give them the space and time they need to express themselves, and then work together to solve the problem.

Another way patience comes into play is with yourself. You need to be patient with yourself as you try this new approach. If these skills are new to you, don't expect to master them the first time you use them. Even the most skilled communicators still have conversations where using the skills doesn't go well. Don't let a few struggles get in your way of moving on and trying again. Do not see these times as failures because they are learning opportunities. Take what went well and do more and identify what didn't go well and make the changes needed so that over time you see and feel the powerful difference it makes for your child and your relationship!

*Silence.* There are times, no matter who you are chatting

with, that silences makes an appearance. As a listener, this can be uncomfortable and make it difficult to know what to do. We live in a busy world with constant stimulation fighting for our attention, so we are not used to silence. The discomfort of silence might make us think something is wrong.

Even though it can be uncomfortable, silence can also be a valuable asset in communication. Silence gives your child the time they need to collect their thoughts and say what they want to say. Avoid asking questions during the silence; let them process what you have already asked. Let silence be an ally rather than an enemy to both you and your child.

Make sure that when there is silence, you keep yourself present. Your attention will want to wander, and when that happens, your body language will change. Remember, people are sensitive to changes in body language. Your child will notice when you look away, start fidgeting or check your watch. This will close the door to them speaking with you. Keep yourself engaged so that your body language shows your child you are still with them!

### The Difference of Communicating like a HERO

Let's take a look at two different dialogues between a father and son. In one, the father is *reacting* to the situation rather than listening. The second example is of a father listening to their child like a HERO and trying some of the communication skills. To give context for the examples, this father was approached by his ten-year-old son, who got in trouble at school for hitting a student. Check it out and see if you can spot what works and what does not and any similarities to your approach.

### Example #1: Reacting to the Situation

Son: Dad, I have something to give you. (Nervous/anxious about what his dad will do)

Dad: What is it, son?

Son: It's a note from school.

Dad: What did you do? Give it to me. (Frustration building, the *reaction* is starting)

Son: I didn't do anything! (Getting defensive to dad's reaction)

Dad: Don't tell me you didn't; they don't just give a note like this for nothing! I've told you not to hit other kids; you know better than this! (*Reacting* more, not giving any room for explanation)

Son: You told me to stick up for myself (Not feeling heard and starting to turn against his dad)

Dad: I told you to do well in school, not get into fights! (Defending himself)

Son: This is ridiculous! (Disconnect growing between father and son)

Dad: No, the fight was ridiculous! You're grounded for a month, and if there is any more of this at school, you'll have a price to pay! (Threats coming from *reacting*)

Son: That's not fair! (Feels defeated and disconnected as the relational bank account drains)

Dad: You should have thought of that before hitting someone! Now get to your room; I can't believe this!

Son: Fine! (Feels unheard and no longer on the same team with his dad)

So, what happened in this dialogue? We have a son nervous about getting into a fight at school and what his dad will do about it. The dad's reactivity justifies his nerves as he feels immediate judgment and blame from his dad, asking, "what did you do?" The conversation from that point becomes one-sided, with the dad using accusations and drawing on his authority to decide what happened and what he will do about it. There is no discussion, just reactions.

The son most likely approached the dad already nervous from what happened, and who wouldn't, especially if this is the pattern? These nerves and fears were quickly validated as the dad reacted only. Once his dad began to react, so did the son by becoming defensive. His voice was silenced rapidly, and all he could do was protest with anger. Each word the dad and son used was a withdrawal from their relational account. Instead of moving the situation forward, this father and son went backward. Neither side was listening, and nothing productive was accomplished. Let's see how different it goes when we listen like a HERO!

### Example #2: Listening like a HERO

Son: Dad, I have something to give you. (Nervous/anxious about what his dad will do)

Dad: What is it, son?

Son: It's a note from school.

Dad: A note from school, that must be making you a bit nervous (Empathy/validating feeling)

Son: I am dad, and I'm sorry. (Feeling validated, still nervous)

Dad: (takes a deep breath as he takes the note) It seems something happened at school today.

Son: Yes. (Heart racing, growing nervous)

Dad: It must be hard to talk about. (Empathy)

Son: Yes. (Nervous but feeling some relief dad is not getting mad)

Dad: The note here says you got in a fight with another student. What does the note not tell me about what happened? (Clear Picture Question)

Son: There was a boy picking on me, and he said some awful things. (Safety is being built, which allows him to feel safe to speak to his dad)

Dad: It hurts when people say awful things about us. (Empathy)

Son: It did hurt! And it made me mad! I did what you told me to do; I defended myself! (Continues feeling safe enough to talk)

Dad: That's not quite what I meant. (Dad feels a bit defensive)

Son: How was I supposed to know?!? (Goes on the defensive hearing dad's tone)

Dad: (takes a quick breath to regroup) Hmm, that is tough. You were just trying to take care of yourself. (Realizing he took a step back, dad uses empathy and paraphrasing to get back on track)

Son: It is tough! I'm sorry dad, I didn't mean to get in trouble! (Feeling safety returning)

Dad: I know, son. It is hard when someone calls us names;

it feels awful. What else is missing from this note? (Empathy, paraphrasing, and Clear Picture Question)

Interestingly, we have the same father and son, and yet this conversation went very differently. In the first example, the dad went straight for the *reaction* and ended up taking a withdrawal from the relationship. In the second example, the dad showed his son respect through a willingness to listen. This created space and security for his son to speak rather than defend himself. When we create space and security for our children, they are more likely to be open with us.

The father used several different skills, sometimes together, to help build that space and security. There was paraphrasing to help ensure he understood what his son was saying. Empathy helped the dad level with his son's emotional experience, especially when bringing the problem up. Clear Picture Questions filled in the blanks with information rather than the dad's assumptions. How much difference did this approach make it for his son compared to the first example?

For the son, his nerves were validated, the pain he was experiencing was heard, and he felt the space and safety and was able to speak his mind. Will this happen each time? Of course not, there will still be times that our children do not open up fully. Just remember that the more security you provide, the more likely your child will open up. As you can see from the example, as dads, we need to press pause on our views and assumptions and give our child a chance. We will get the opportunity to speak and problem-solve; just don't do it too early, or you'll close off that space and security.

The hard part about putting communication into a book

is I can't show you the body language that was going on in either example. Body language is essential to communication and accounts for a lot more of our message's quality than the words we say. A quick review of each example allows us to predict the father and son's probable body language.

In the first example, when the father begins to *react* rather than listen, what might his body language look like? Maybe there was finger-pointing, tightly folded arms, or standing up and looking down at the child. Not exactly the type of postures that create space and safety for a child.

If that was the father's body language, what might the child be doing? Perhaps the son crossed his arms, leaned away from his dad to try and get space, or threw his arms up in defeat. The body language of one influences the other. With the dad *reacting* to the situation in general, he will probably get more worked up when he feels his son trying to disengage by the boy's body language. It is not hard to see how this body language makes the situation worse, and nothing positive or constructive gets done.

What might the body language look like in the second example? In this situation, the father immediately created space and safety through empathy and concern. His body language might have helped with this by maintaining positive eye contact, putting an empathetic hand on a shoulder, sitting at the same level, and not crossing any parts of his body. This creates an alignment between his words and his actions.

For the son, seeing this body language would only reinforce the space and security. The son was nervous, and it probably showed when he came in with his head down.

When his father kept a calm demeanor and his words and posture aligned, it created space and security for the son to start opening up. The son was able to interact with his dad about what happened. You can do this exact thing for your children!

Listening like a HERO takes time, effort, and patience. We must value providing this type of security for our children and see the worth in doing so. When we mess up during the listening process, go back to the basics of listening to get that security back. Take a moment to gauge your readiness to listen like a HERO. Is there anywhere you need to continue practicing and growing? Put in the work and watch your relationship transform!

## Final Thoughts

When it comes to communication, just know there is always something new to learn and try out. As you try out new things, remember that you will not always see how effective they are in the first go-round. If the first time you give it a go it does not work, do not see that as proof it will never work. Trying out new things changes the pattern and creates resistance. Keep going and refining your approach. Rarely does anyone get a new skill down in their first few tries, so be patient and ready to try numerous times!

An important fact about communication is you are only able to control yourself. When your message is not coming across, look at your delivery and presentation. If you do not change anything, your communication pattern will start to feel like a movie scene that goes the same way every time. If you and your children are stuck in this loop, chances are you are getting stuck on content rather than looking at the process of how you communicate.

If you focus on the process, you can stop the loop because you will try something else. When you are stuck in a loop with your child, the only one you can control is you. That is where using these tools come in; they change the game and break the loop. Take the time to assess how you currently communicate, how effective it is in the short and long-term, and what changes can be made so you can build a strong relationship.

Communication is essential to everything you will do as a father. There is no escaping it, and there are no cutting corners. Positive communication provides some of the largest deposits you can make into your relational bank account with your children. You can validate your children, build up their self-worth and self-confidence, teach them about compassion, show them forgiveness, and so much more through the way you communicate.

The process of communication will look different for each of your children. The more you get to know them and their uniqueness, the more you will learn their style and adapt your process to them. Learn how your body language impacts each child or the way you say things. More than anything, remember to listen like a HERO to each of your children. You will be surprised by the results and how different you feel about your child. That will build a foundation for a strong relationship where your children will want to come to you when they need you most. Now, go be their HERO!

# | 10 |

# Looking for Balance

This chapter is about balance. No, we are not talking yoga balancing here; we are talking about three major life balances. We will explore the balance between being a father and a friend, which can be a tough balance to strike! Second, we'll look at a work-life balance to help us manage our roles in and outside of the home. Finally, the balance of personal time and responsibilities will be examined.

When we feel balanced in our lives, it feels like we are flowing and things get done without burning out. It's almost like we are in such a groove that the effort is not overly strenuous. The times we feel out of balance is a much different experience. We may try to say that we fee fine, but eventually, something will give. As soon as that happens, there is a cost that we face personally and with our families.

Finding a balance does not mean we devote equal time to every role in our lives. There will be times when you are giving more energy to your home and family, and sometimes it will be at work or school. A balance means finding the groove that works best for you and your family. It means identifying your roles and responsibilities and setting yourself and your family up for success as you take care of your duties. Let's start with the first balance we must strike, which is crucial to your effectiveness as a father.

## Father and Friend

A common discussion with the dads I have worked with is whether we should be a father or a friend first. You might have had that question come into your head as you've read this book. A balance between being a father and a friend means a couple of things. The father's side of this balance looks at the ability to coach and mentor your children, set limits, provide consequences, and enduring the struggles of watching your children struggle. I've worked with many fathers who fear this side of the balance because they do not want to put a power dynamic in play with their children. This side of the balance also requires your time, effort, and energy without immediate gratification.

Being a friend, the other side of the balance, means you're more concerned about playing a friend's role, rescuing them, having fun, and seeing yourself and your child in the relationship as equals. The emphasis of being a friend is not done with bad intent, as these fathers want their children to grow up on their own volition, pursue their own wants and desires, and not fear their father. Also, sometimes being a friend is easier and more fun for the dad.

The goal of this balance is not only to have one side or the other. Remember, this chapter is about balance, which means finding the right blend of being a father AND a friend. As a dad, just know that your responsibilities are first as a father. This is a powerful responsibility, and it must be embraced before taking on a friend's role. We'll break this down as we move forward.

A healthy combination of father and friend is incredibly beneficial for our children. It's when that balance goes out of whack that there will start to be issues. Too much emphasis on the father part increases the focus on boundaries and discipline and lowers the chance for fun and connection. In contrast, too much friend means focusing only on the fun stuff and not putting in the structure and mentoring that children need to thrive.

Before we move too much further in this discussion, I want you to connect to your initial thoughts and reactions to what we have discussed so far. Reflect on your initial thoughts and the following questions to see what you are thinking and feeling about this topic. What are my views on the father and friend balance? Which end of the balance do I operate from most of the time, and why? How is it working out for my child and me currently? Are any changes needed, and if so, what changes are they?

Hopefully, you have a better grip on where you are at with this balance so far. Your balance will look unique to you, and only you will know if there are needed changes. Keep these thoughts in mind and see if anything changes as we move through the next part of breaking down two different versions of this balance.

### Friend Then Father

A common struggle dads have brought up to me is feeling like they are too much of a friend first, so that is where we will start. The friend side tends to take the authority dynamic out of the equation, so our children see us as friends rather than a power-hungry man who just wants control. By being a friend first, the hope is that by changing the power dynamic, our children will be more willing to trust us and come to us with their problems. This helps us feel like the cool parent, the chill one that our children always want to be around.

There are many different reasons why one might approach their relationship with their child in this way. Some may have grown up with fathers who exemplify the power-hungry and controlling dad and struggled to grow in an environment with verbal and physical threats. For dads who grew up in this type of environment, they may have vowed to do the complete opposite so they don't put their children through that. To not be like their father, they approach their child's relationship from the friend angle rather than the father one first.

Another potential reason is the father not wanting to interfere with their child as they grow up. What does that mean? Our culture has increased emphasis on letting children grow up to be who they want to be with minimal interference. Acting as a friend makes it easier for dads to stay out of their children's way as they navigate their world. The dad does not want to put up any roadblocks that the child would have to overcome. This frees the child up to become whoever they want to become.

A third common reason to focus on the friend side of the balance is pain aversion. Being a father comes with pain, and I am not just talking about the physical pain of a toddler turning the corner at a full sprint right into your groin! The times we have to discipline or see our child struggle, hurt, or fail creates pain for us. To prevent this, the dad takes on the friend role to keep their child out of pain. In essence, the father wants to avoid their own pain while also keeping their child from hurting.

A four reason could be one that is a little more subconscious and runs in the background. The friend role gives the impression of making fatherhood easier. Instead of holding the child to a limit, coaching them through a challenging emotional experience, or teaching them to solve a problem, it's easier to say "let's go play" or "here's a treat." It helps us avoid pain, get out of the child's way, and prevents us from acting in a way that reminds us of our controlling fathers. Of course, being a dad was never meant to be easy, and it will only become more demanding if we act like water and take the path of least resistance, but more on that in just a moment.

This is not an exhaustive list of reasons why a dad might choose being a friend over a father first. For example, maybe the dad is filling a need for having companionship. Perhaps they do not feel competent in their tools and knowledge of what the father's side of the balance requires. No matter the reason, you need to reflect on your identity as a father and see if you approach it from the Friend then Father approach. To help illustrate why you should do this, let's look at potential outcomes with the Friend then Father approach.

**Outcomes of Friend Then Father.** A question you might have on your mind is what is wrong with being a friend first. Research has consistently found that children have better life outcomes when they grow up in a home where predictable boundaries are consistently enforced. As these children mature and demonstrate maturity in handling responsibility and freedom, the structure needs to adjust and provide more opportunities for continued growth. If we draw on the fishing metaphor from the control chapter, the outcomes are better when there is enough tension on the line balanced with slack to provide freedom.

Approaching the relationship from a friend-first perspective will not have this balance of tension and slack on the line, and you are more likely to see a lot of line piling on the water. The more we act like just a friend, the harder it will be to reel things back in with our children. There will be too much slack on the water to get the right amount of tension needed to reel it in.

Some fathers have argued for being a friend first by looking at the relational bank account. The thought is that being a fun dad builds up the account balance to high levels. Unfortunately, research indicates that it is more of a pseudo-deposit that comes with a catch. While having a lot of fun with our children does create deposits, the lack of structure and consistent leadership leads to hidden fees. What does that mean?

Relationships need trust and respect to be effective. Trust and respect come from fun times and, more importantly, the tough times for our children. Though our children do not like to be disciplined, when we follow through on what we say we are going to do and use positive and respectful discipline, we create trust.

As our children grow and experience the struggles of adolescence, they will begin to look more closely at the relationship they have with us. If it is built strictly on fun, chances are they will not take us seriously with the more formidable struggles because we haven't built up the trust that we will be there in the hard times. Instead of the balance in our relational bank account remaining high, resentment and insecurity in our abilities to be there for them when it matters most causes hidden fees that drain the balance.

Another pattern you might see in a friend-first relationship is the child learning they can get anything from their parent. This leads to entitlement and a power imbalance. The child takes all the power in the relationship and turns the parent into a means to an end. Again, the account's balance is not healthy because it acts more like a credit card. There is the appearance that you have funds, but in reality, the funds are loaned, and you pay dearly for any credit balance.

While some fathers and children navigate this well, the reality is that fathering strictly from the friend-first perspective makes the journey that much more difficult. You increase the chances for stormy seas for an adventure that already has enough obstacles. We think we might make it easier for our children to come to us by being friends first; however, it is quite often the opposite. Let's see what happens when we flip this around and start as a father with the right amount of friend.

**Father then Friend**

Empowered Fathers act as both a father and friend by drawing on the strengths that come with both constructs. When we act as a father first, we ensure that we teach and prepare our children for life while building our relationship with them. We put a structure in place in our homes with rules and expectations and consequences and learning opportunities that uphold it. We help teach our children to problem-solve their issues and manage the ebbs and flows of life.

Acting as a father first means we let our children struggle at times to help them build resilience and persistence. That does not mean there is no support and guidance because we are there when they need us most. The difference is we do not do everything and solve all our children's problems. At times this does create withdrawals from our relationship; however, we build trust and respect because we are there in the tough times and have done our part to help them learn the tools they need to survive. This creates a strong and lasting connection with our children.

To balance out the structure and discipline that comes with the father dimension, Empowered Fathers draw on the friend dynamic. This lets our children see we are human and can have a good time too. If we focus only on the father side, we may find ourselves continually disciplining and feeling distant from our children. That is not enjoyable for you or your children! If you find yourself in this rut, it's time to turn to the friend part of the balance!

Being a friend to our child means spending time with them, getting to know who they are and what they value in life. When coupled appropriately with the father dimension, being a friend helps build and solidify strong relationships with your children. It provides the foundation of trust and security necessary for the more challenging topics that come up as our children grow older. It creates predictability for our children in how we will behave and approach them. What does having a balance of father and then friend do for the future?

**Outcomes of Father then Friend.** Finding a working balance between Father and Friend is one way to ensure your child grows up with a strong relationship with you. Having a predictable environment that enforces limits positively while also encouraging problem-solving and life skill development is optimal for children. This environment also needs to embrace their natural curiosity and inclination to play, a prime place for the Friend side to come in!

As a father, enforcing your home's structure positively and constructively keeps the dignity of your child and yourself intact. Your child will learn to understand the limits of their behavior, which creates a sense of security because they know where the boundaries are. The bonus is that it prepares them for adulthood's limitations like jobs and living within their means. When you use your home as a training ground for real life by using the Father side of the balance, your children will have a higher likelihood of successfully managing their future life.

Drawing on the power of Friend also comes with short and long-term benefits. In the short-term, you will feel the connection you share while having good times together. For most dads, the fun side is something that comes easy. We like to play anyways, so getting the chance to do that with our children lets us feel like a child again too! When your children see you having a blast with them, it boosts their sense of worth. It fulfills their need to belong and be connected with you, and your relational bank account is where you'll see the benefit of this treasured time!

The long-term benefits include your children growing up knowing that you will be there for them through the good and bad. When life gets tough, and your children are introduced to drugs, sex, alcohol, skipping school, and all the other crazy temptations, they know you will be there. Your relational bank account with them will be strong enough that they feel they can come to you with those challenges. Having the lighter side of Friend helps balance out Father's firmness and structure. Both ends of the balance work synergistically through time and experience to help your children know you will be there.

Another long-term benefit of balancing Father and then Friend is it will help your relationship with each child adapt appropriately over time. The relationship you have with your children when they are eight should not look the same when they are sixteen. You must be flexible as your children learn and grow and start to follow the path they choose for their life. If you act strictly from the Father's side, this flexibility may come slower if at all. Having flexibility means your relationship will grow in ways that leave communication channels open and let your child fully embrace their vision for their life.

Finding this balance as time moves forward and your children grow is no easy feat. Each of your children is unique, and you can't always prepare for what they will face. You are learning on the fly every day! Going back to the fishing line metaphor, you want to make sure there is a nice combo of slack and tension on the line. This will help you decide to reel in or step back as your children try out different ideas and experiences!

Before we move on to the next balance, take some time to reflect on being a Father and Friend. How close are you to the balance you want? Which role would you say you go with first usually? What changes need to be made? What will you keep doing because it is working so well? Do not wait; there is no better time than now to find the balance!

### Finding a Work-Life Balance

A balance that always needs fine-tuning and changing is the work-life balance. There has been a call in our world to find a work-life balance to promote a healthy lifestyle. Maintaining a positive work-life balance helps strengthen our families as we spend quality time together, making deposits into each relationship. Striking a work-life balance is a complicated process, and I would encourage you to research beyond this section. There are many different ideas and strategies about this balance beyond this book's scope; don't hesitate to get out there and explore a bit!

Let's talk about a few things that can get in the way of having a work-life balance. As fathers, we tend to put a lot of the responsibility to provide for our families on ourselves. Bringing economic stability to our family allows us to feel like we have fulfilled a key part of our role as a father.

It is easy to get lost in economic responsibility and go too far. If we are working hard to provide for our families, that is a noble undertaking. If we are spending too much time at work, we need to ask ourselves what the cost is of doing this when it comes to our children and the relationships we have with them. Too much of a focus on finances leads us to neglect the most essential accounts we have. We need to make sure that we provide regular deposits into our relational bank accounts with our children, and the most vital way to do this is the time we spend with them.

When we become a father, we take on different responsibilities that have more weight than ever before. With the many fathers I have worked with, being a provider is the one they take on the most as that seems to be the socially-accepted norm for males. Finding a work-life balance puts us to the task of identifying the other important ways we provide to our families beyond finances.

Fathers provide emotional security and help meet the needs of their children. You will be able to do this more effectively when you balance your work responsibilities with those you have at home. This balance collapses when we put too much emphasis on one side or the other. Putting too much weight on one side of the balance automatically takes away from the other.

One thing to keep in mind when striking this balance is time. There are 168 hours in a week; that's a fact we can't change. We may not be able to change the amount of time in a week, but we can change how we manage and use that time. When you look at your work-life balance, do not think it means putting the same number of hours into each of your responsibilities. That is simply unrealistic! Though the time may not equal the same amount, that does not mean the quality of time you spend with your child won't make up for that. The times you are with your child and engaged in their world is more effective than merely the amount of time alone.

When you are at work, for the most part, that is where your emphasis and focus should lie. When you return home, try and leave work outside the door as much as possible. This can be hard to do, especially when a day has been incredibly stressful, and you hear screaming as soon as you put your hand on your door. The key to work-life balance is making the time meaningful for each of the roles you have. Sometimes that means looking at our personal time and how we manage that with our responsibilities.

## Personal Time and Responsibilities

Personal time is a powerful part of a fulfilling life as long as we are doing it when it is appropriate versus when it is not. We live in a time where technology permeates every part of our lives, including parenting. How often have you pulled your phone out to read a text or play a game while sitting on the floor with your child "playing" trucks?

What do your children typically do when you pull out your phone? How many sighs have you heard? Does your child try to wrestle your phone away or start acting up? If you have more than one child, do they fight or act up to get your attention? No matter how secretive you are trying to be, your children notice. They are concerned that they are not important to you and that you would rather focus on your phone.

Since our phones are one way we try and get personal time, we need to ask ourselves how important is what we are doing on our phone when we are with our children. Can we wait ten minutes to check out that notification? In most cases, the answer is yes, we can definitely wait. It is a choice to use your phone, not a necessity. You can make an easy deposit into the relational bank account by just putting your phone away for a few minutes to be present in the moment with your child. If you choose not to, it makes a withdrawal from the account just as quickly.

The more you pull your phone out, the more it reinforces your child's fear that you are more concerned about your phone than them. While it may only be a few minutes at a time, this adds up. If you are looking at your phone for two or three minutes at a time when you are with your children and do this ten times a day, you miss out on a half-hour of quality time with your children. The more this occurs, the more time you lose to your screen and the more disconnected your child feels. You only get this time once; make it count!

Personal time is vital to your overall health. Ensure that your personal time recharges your batteries, re-centers you, and moves you towards peace and calm. Do your personal care at a time that respects others present, such as your partner or children. Do not just disappear on them; let them know what you need, your plan for accomplishing it, and when you'll be done. If you are currently in a relationship, keep in mind the power of giving your partner the time they need to engage in personal time as well. You will both be more effective when your personal time and responsibilities are in balance!

## Final Thoughts

Remember that finding a balance in your life is a process rather than a destination. It is up to you to be flexible enough to accommodate the day's needs with your responsibilities. This requires you to engage in self-assessment to find a balance in your life. Honesty with yourself is critical. If something is not working, admit it so you can find a way to make it work. Otherwise, you might spread your efforts too thin and feel like you do not see any flow in your life. An honest self-assessment will allow you to realize where you are putting too much effort and where you are ineffective. If needed, take the time to research these topics more to help you more. Finding a flow and balance in life will make things more manageable and allow you to be the best father you can be!

# | 11 |

# Mom and the Empowered Father

This book has focused intensely on you, but for this chapter, we will move that focus to the relationship you have with the mother of your children. For some, this might be a divisive topic, whereas others may not see it as a big deal. As we move through this discussion, we will look at the two variations of parenting together in the same home and co-parenting.

It would be unreasonable to believe that this final chapter can address everything regarding working with mom. In reality, I hope to give a few insightful thoughts and tips when it comes to the relationship you have with the mother of your children. If you father with a fellow dad, make any needed changes or adaptations to the tips to help your relationship.

Depending on your situation, this could be a challenging chapter that might lead you to feel anger, frustration, defiance, or hopelessness. If the relationship with mom has deteriorated to the point of no return, it can be hard to see a reason to keep trying.

Just know that once you have a child together, you will always be parents together. It may look different based on circumstances, but you will always be part of one another's life in some capacity. Due to this, you and mom need to find a way to raise your child collaboratively for the child's benefit. All that I ask of you for this chapter is to continue having an open mind and see if there are any thoughts or ideas that work for you.

## Values and Mom

### Parenting Together

Mothers play an important role in children's development. You must assess your values about mom and her role in raising the children. How much do you value her views, believes, and actions around motherhood and the structure in the home? Valuing mom and her unique and powerful role in the home will model a positive relationship for your children. It teaches your children to value their mom as they see you value her. If they see you disrespecting, putting down, or treating mom negatively, your children might try to do the same thing. Set the bar high by valuing mom and your combined contributions as parents.

One question I challenge you to consider is how you are showing that you do value her. Many of us intuitively know that we value mom, but we do not take the time to let her know what we value regularly. Remember, values are something of worth to us. Let your partner know what it is you value and her!

## Co-Parenting

Depending on how the circumstances are currently in your co-parenting situation, you might be thinking either that valuing mom will be easy or that it just might be impossible. Even if the relationship is in a bitter place, there is still a reason to value her. She is the mother of your children, and that will not change.

If it seems to you that valuing her may be impossible, take the time to work through the following questions. What are the biggest obstacles getting in the way of being able to value her role as mom? What might be the potential consequences, both positive and negative, if you do not value her as a mom? What behaviors on your part would need to change to show that you value her? What are the outcomes for each of your children you co-parent if you continue this way? How would the outcomes differ if you make the needed changes?

I have worked with many dads that say it is not their behavior but their ex that needs to change. This is an easy trap to fall into, and it does nothing positive for your children. Let's face it; chances are your ex is also waiting for you to change. If you are waiting for her and she is waiting for you, what do you think the chances are that anything will change for the positive?

Taking that first step to show that you value her enough as the mother of your children does not mean that you are giving in, admitting you were wrong unless you need to, or that you are less of a man. Raising your children in a co-parenting relationship is a marathon. If you are both still blaming and waiting for the other person to change, you might as well do the marathon wearing cement shoes. Taking the first step to valuing her role as a mom means you can get moving again. This will make more sense as we continue to work our way through the other concepts in the chapter.

## Emotions and Mom

### Parenting Together

Typically, men and women were raised differently when it comes to emotions. It is not uncommon for men to get the message that emotions are weak, shove them down, and that men do not cry. Women are typically raised to discuss their feelings, have them be guides, and experience and work through their emotional conflict. With these contrasting views, it is not surprising that emotions can get in the way of a parental team being effective when emotions run high.

As you learn to understand better and manage your emotions, you open new doors in the relationship you have with your partner. While emotions may seem like a waste of time to some, they are powerful connectors that attach us to our partners. Being comfortable with our emotional experience allows us to recognize and validate the emotions of our partner. This creates valuable deposits into your relational bank account with your partner, which is a winning recipe!

Parenting comes with stressful moments that will test your ability to regulate yourself. Children are adept at hitting the hot spots at the wrong times, creating emotional *reactions* that make the situation worse rather than better. This same thing goes on for mom. Being there for your partner by helping them work through their emotions increases the likelihood that they will be there when you need them. They keep you connected as a team rather than feelings pulling you apart.

Conflict, which we will discuss later in the chapter, is one place emotions come into play. Being an Empowered Father means learning to accept your emotions and manage them in respectful and healthy ways to yourself and those around you. During conflict, seek to create connection with your emotions rather than division. As your partner experiences intense emotions, go for collaboration rather than competition. This is a much different approach that will take time, patience, and practice to master. However, your family will benefit from both of you making this happen!

Being open to emotions can strengthen your relationship with your partner. This comes in handy when navigating the challenging waters of parenting that inevitably come at times. Your children will benefit from seeing their parents manage their emotions while working together. You will promote healthy emotional regulation and teamwork that your children will incorporate into their lives and relationships as well!

### Co-Parenting

Emotions are a complicated topic when it comes to co-parenting. If you are struggling with your former partner, you may feel justified in letting your anger out. While this may feel good momentarily, it typically does incredible damage to the co-parenting relationship in the long run. This damage pushes you further away from working together well enough for your children to have healthy outcomes. In essence, it comes back and harms your child.

Discussions with former partners over parenting decisions have been described by some fathers I've worked with as a "warzone." In other words, emotions are present and typically out of control, which leads to intense conflict that creates more damage and never solves anything. Our children become collateral damage in this type of conflict, which we do not always think about at the moment.

As an Empowered Father, you need to take the time to work through your emotions regarding your former partner. This means working through perceived injustices, blame, the loss of the relationship, and perceived power differences. This may require a professional to help promote new understandings of yourself and the state of your affairs. Both partners can't sit around waiting for the other to change; someone has to take a step forward to change the game that will impact your children. Why not you?

When looking at your co-parenting relationship, what types of things bring up emotional reactions for you? What emotions do you typically feel, and what are they communicating to you? What areas do you feel you have a handle on where is there room for improvement in managing your emotions around your co-parent? Working through these questions and revisiting the emotions chapter is an excellent start to using emotions in a constructive manner that builds your child's future up through your co-parenting relationship. Be patient with the process, and be brave as you move forward on that journey!

## Control and Mom

### Parenting Together

Control is difficult enough to manage as just a father, but it can complicate things when two parents are involved. Both of you will need to work together to find ways to ensure that each person can maintain their sense of control while forming a unified parental team. What does that mean? As a parental team, both of you need to work together to enforce the home's structure.

When children see their parents as a unified front, it can help build trust and security. Both you and your partner are equal in power and back one another up. If one tries to hoard the power, that destroys the ability to work together. That comes when one intentionally undermines the other, such as when one parent says no, so the other says yes.

As a couple, discuss your needs and beliefs around control. Now that you have taken the time to learn about yourself as a father and your relationship with control, you are more equipped with what you need to talk with your partner. Be open to hearing your partner's needs and beliefs while working collaboratively to ensure these needs are being met for each of you.

If you and your partner find yourselves at odds over parenting often, control is an excellent place to start. Remember, you are equal partners with equal power. Use each other's strengths and work together to find a balance to help maintain control in the home. Children will thrive in a home where control gets shared amongst the parents and with the children!

### Co-Parenting

Control in a co-parenting relationship can be a sensitive topic to discuss. Often, both parents want to know what is going on in the other household and have influence over it. Control is one of the most challenging obstacles to overcome in the co-parenting relationship. It is not uncommon for each partner to use control to get back at the other. Unfortunately, it is not just your relationship with the co-parent that struggles since your children get stuck in the middle.

Children often get turned into spies for parents and are asked to report what goes on in the other household. Not surprisingly, these children are more likely to grow up experiencing higher rates of anxiety, depression, and relationship struggles than their peers who are not in this situation. Everything you and your co-parent do or don't do will impact your children.

You need to identify what control means to you in the context of your co-parenting relationship. You do have control over your home and the rules that you put in place. That control does not extend to your co-parent's home. You can control your responses to your children's discussion of your former partner. In essence, the only control you have is over yourself and the environment you help create.

Take a moment to reflect on control. How might you

be attempting to overextend your control? In what ways is control helping or hindering your co-parenting relationship? What impacts are you having on your children with you manage control? Take an honest look at control and its role in your co-parenting relationship because the quality of your children's life depends on it!

## Perceptions and Mom

### Parenting Together

When working with mom, you need to know how you think about her and what she does. Some of us may feel that we are incredibly lucky because our partners are amazing mothers who seem to know just what to do. Others may think that mom is too permissive and lets children get away with murder. Perhaps you feel she's too strict. You need to identify what your perceptions are for the same reasons you need to about your children. The way you see your partner is how you will treat them. It guides your responses and reactions to their behavior and words. If your perceptions are distorted, your interpretations of the situation and actions in response will be too.

The goal in identifying your perceptions of mom is not so you can mold her into what you think she should be. She does not want that any more than you would like that from her! Instead, the goal is to look at her realistically, which helps you understand why she might do things the way she does. You want to see her in a way that builds her up and increases your parental team's effectiveness. If both of you actively build one another up, it only helps the team!

One way to identify your perception is to think about the standard you hold her against. Look at the image in your head of what a mother should be that you have put together from your own mother or experiences with others. Assess whether or not it is a realistic standard. If you compare your partner to an unrealistic standard, you are putting them at a disadvantage and opening the door to conflict and struggle that doesn't need to be there.

If needed, take the time to edit the picture you have of your partner. Here's a tip to do that: focus on her strengths and the observable things she does. This will help you work together on the same team rather than as two opposing teams facing off. Sometimes it is our perceptions that are the roadblock to an effective parental team!

### Co-Parenting

Depending on the co-parent relationship's quality, your perceptions of mom could range from honest and realistic to negatively skewed. If the relationship ended on a bitter note, it is not uncommon for each partner to blame the other for what happened. When this occurs, the other person becomes the image of what is wrong and gets labeled as selfish, unreasonable, and the one to blame. It is not hard to see why having these perceptions does not help the co-parenting.

If you get stuck in these perceptions of your former partner, there is no way you will be able to navigate the co-parenting relationship well enough to help your children out.

Co-parenting needs to be about the children and helping them towards their best outcome possible. It is not about you and your former partner settling old scores. When this happens, it is the child who is on the losing end every time.

There can be the perception that mom has all the power, and there is little you can do to influence anything. If you feel small and insignificant in the co-parenting relationship, then you will respond that way. You may close yourself off from the idea of challenging the status quo and bringing up your struggles and concerns. Of course, nothing will change if this is how you approach the situation!

If you and mom see each other as immovable, chances are things will either stay the same or deteriorate further. Being humble and open to seeing your former partner in a different light for your children's sake is necessary. Someone has to take the first step for change to happen. There is a chance there, so take it, don't sit and wait.

To begin challenging some of your perceptions, here are a few questions to consider. How fair is the picture in my head of my former partner? How realistic are my views of the co-parent, and what evidence do I have for the good and the bad? How are my behavior, reactions, and responses influencing my co-parenting to act in specific ways? It can be hard to see a co-parent realistically, especially if the relationship ended bitterly. The fact is your children will benefit greatly from a working co-parenting relationship and it helps create more positive outcomes. This can happen, especially if you change the way you see your co-parent.

## Modeling and Mom

### Parenting Together

Modeling provides a way to show your partner the changes you have made in your journey as an Empowered Father. By responding rather than reacting to your partner, you will be demonstrating new ways of doing things. You will show your partner and children what is important to you through your actions. It is amazing how your partner and children will try similar things when they see and feel the results of your work. We can't control people; we can only influence them!

Having a strong team with mom models a healthy relationship for your children. Your children will learn about relationships from your relationship with your partner. They will learn about teamwork and overcoming challenges with their future partners by the example you model. Let your relationship be a powerful form of intentional modeling that sets their future relationships up for success!

### Co-Parenting

If you have chosen to take the first step in creating a new path for your co-parenting relationship, modeling will be a crucial part of your success. The way you communicate, respond rather than *react*, handle your emotions, discuss your views and beliefs, and maintain control of yourself will do a few things for your co-parent. First, it models to them that your behavior aligns with the changes you are making. Second, it creates safety over time, as long as you continue in your new pattern. Third, it provides a model for your former partner on what they can do differently to help the relationship run smoothly enough to parent together for your children.

This does not mean that you will have power over them because you show them a new way. That is the absolute opposite thing you are going for here, and if it comes off that way, nothing will change. Instead, your example can help provide a new path for your relationship and the freedom for your co-parent to decide what they will do differently. When you are empathetic, validating, and open, your former partner will likely do the same in a way that works for them over time.

The relationship you have with your co-parent becomes part of the template your children will form in their heads and use for their future relationships. If you deal with conflict through yelling, disrespect, aggression, and criticizing one another, your child is more likely to do this to solve their disagreements. This makes co-parenting a challenging relationship to manage, but it can be done!

It is up to you and your co-parent to decide the type of relationship you want to model for your children. You can help model how to overcome disagreements, give and take healthily and constructively, and show how to love your children regardless of the circumstances. The way you and your co-parent navigate your relationship will impact your children's quality of relationships in the future.

Think about your co-parenting relationship. What do you believe as the father you are modeling for your children? What steps can you take to improve on what you are modeling? What do you hope you are teaching your children about relationships through the example you model with your co-parent? What might be your fears for what you are teaching? Modeling is a powerful tool; for good or bad, it's up to you and your co-parent to decide what it will do for your children.

## Communication and Mom

### Parenting Together

Communication allows you and your partner to exchange thoughts, ideas, and beliefs to bring you closer or create distance in your parental team. The more open you are in your communication, the more likely you are to work together efficiently. Remember listening like a HERO? Use it with your partner to keep your relationship healthy and functioning at a high level!

Listening to your partner is critical. Don't worry; you will still have your turn to talk. Listening to your partners will make the times you do get to speak more effective because people that feel heard by you are more likely to listen and respond positively to you. As you're listening, validate their experience, paraphrase what you have heard, and be genuinely interested in their views. When your partner feels validated, heard, and understood, they are more likely to do the same for you. Make sure to have an open line of communication with your partner. Use your communication to help you work as a team. We'll cover a few tips for having hard conversations in just a moment since that can be a tricky part of communication.

### Co-Parenting

Being in a co-parenting relationship will impact communication frequency, but it does not have to keep you from being a HERO. In a co-parenting relationship, you have to have a line of communication that focuses on the child, which doesn't always make communication an easy thing to do. Depending on your relationship's quality, one or both of you may not be that interested in hearing what the other has to say. If that continues, what will be the consequence of this for your children?

Being a HERO when listening to your co-parent does not mean you are giving in or letting them win. The hope is that a new cycle can be created in the relationship that will help your children. No matter the differences between you and mom, you have to find a way to work well enough together for your children. You can only control your part in the relationship, which means you need to think about what you want that part to look like and how you will communicate it. Let's take a look at some tips for working through conversations that might be more heated.

### Tips for Tough Conversations with Mom

The following tips and guidelines can be put in place to help navigate more challenging conversations. Work with your partner or co-parent to decide what modifications might be needed for your specific situation. Both of you must commit to having this be a regular part of your communication habits if you want them to work.

1. *Set a time limit.*

   Let's face it, the longer you go when discussing a hot button topic, the more likely you are to end up in a full-blown argument. Set a time limit while keeping in mind that you do not have to solve the entire problem in one sitting. This time limit may be as little as three to five minutes, especially if you and mom typically struggle with conflict. Be flexible and willing to make adjustments. If you start arguing before the time is up, go ahead and stop. You do not have to use the entire time limit.

2. *Stop when productivity is replaced with negativity.*

   How often do things seem to be going well, and then one word or comment pushes the whole thing downhill? When you reach this point, you have a choice. Keep moving forward with negativity leading the way or stop and return to the conversation when it can be productive again. This can be a hard decision to make at the moment if you are feeling wronged or hurt and want to strike back. Resist this temptation because it only creates more harm and pain in the long run. Stop when the negative begins to push the conversation in a negative direction and return when the discussion can be productive.

3. *Get rid of sarcasm and name-calling.*

Discussing hot button topics will make it easier for you to get overheated and turn to sarcasm and name-calling. Men tend to use sarcasm as a way to handle uncomfortable emotions. Unfortunately, sarcasm tends to take a shot at the other person, which likely means productivity will be replaced with negativity. Name-calling makes this worse and is disrespectful to the other person. If you are committed to communicating like a HERO, this stuff has to go!

4. *When one talks, the other listens.*

Tough conversations are not a place to blast one another with different points of view, hoping our volume and intensity will get the point across. These conversations should be a way to grow in understanding of one another, and this can't be done with constant interrupting to throw in your viewpoint. It will be up to you and mom to decide who is talking who is listening, especially at the beginning. Be ready to stop and try again if listening stops or negativity shows up.

5. *Do not bring in the laundry list.*

Discussing challenging topics is an easy way to get you on the defensive as you might feel disrespected or threatened. Defensiveness brings with it the urge to bring out the laundry list of all the wrongs your partner has ever done. This does nothing to help your cause or the relationship and pushes you further away from what you want. If there are things from the past that need addressing, make sure it is part of the issue and brought up respectfully. If the laundry list starts to come out, the conversation is done until both of you have calmed down and are ready to start again.

6. *Focus on Mutual Responsibility instead of Blame*

   This can be a tough one. Focusing on mutual responsibility means talking about how both of you have played a part rather than turning to blame. Instead of saying, "you did this," the language shifts to "I contributed to this by..." A word of caution! It is easy to say something like, "I raised my voice that loud because you weren't listening." You start out sounding like you are focusing on your behavior, but in reality, you are just blaming mom in a roundabout way. Both of you are involved in the situation, and both of you are contributing to the issue. It is not about who is right or wrong; it is about coming to an agreeable solution together.

7. *Give Appreciation.*

   You need to show appreciation to mom, whether working together in the same home or as a co-parent. Giving appreciation creates positivity and trust. When mom discusses something difficult she is going through with your children, share your appreciation for her care and effort. Be specific; otherwise, it comes off as being ingenuine. Being specific means listening intently, and if mom is not expecting appreciation, it can boost your stock as well!

8. *Take a cool-down break when needed.*

If you have reached a point where the conversation is getting heated, and productivity is replaced by negativity, it's time to stop and cool down. Each partner reserves the right to ask for a break to cool down, with the other respecting that wish. When you allow yourself to slow down, you replace irrationality and reactivity with calmness and rational thoughts. Do not ruminate on what is frustrating you during your break; that will lead you to stay wound up and probably bring in the laundry list. When both of you feel calm and ready, start again.

## Final Thoughts

Working with mom will be a powerful part of your fatherhood journey. Regardless of the relationship situation, you need to work together to benefit your child's life unless legal reasons say otherwise. You will be more effective as a father, and she will be more effective as a mother when you can find a way to work as a team. This benefits your children and their future.

As you continue to grow as an Empowered Father, you will learn more about who you are. Take the time to discuss with mom what you are learning. Be open to her feedback. Do not be surprised if she begins to wonder the same things about her. Take the time to listen and learn about who she is. You are working to grow together for your children. Work together as a team instead of opponents where your children will pay the price.

# | 12 |

# Conclusion

An Empowered Father is not some abstract concept or perfect ideal to reach. You are the Empowered Father. You get to mold yourself into the unique man and father you want to be for your children. Your journey is not over. Continue to learn new information and challenge yourself to be better than you were yesterday. More is being asked of us as fathers; it is time for us to step up and knock it out of the park!

Don't forget that the relationship you have with each of your children is the foundation for anything you do. Make deposits regularly and keep withdrawals to a minimum to keep your relational bank account strong. Invest long-term to build the relationship now that you will need when they are older. If your children are already in the adolescent years, your task is to still build the relationship you have now through deposits like listening.

As an Empowered Father, you do not have to know everything. None of us are perfect, and we all must continue to learn and grow. Learn about yourself and how you impact your children. Learn about your children and what they find important in life. Keep in mind when you discipline the relationship and how what you choose to do will impact it.

Continue to learn about your values, beliefs, and perceptions. Examine your needs around control and it helps and hinders you. Explore your emotional experience and identify new ways to manage and regulate yourself. Use intentional modeling to your advantage as you teach your children about life. Communicate like a HERO by being open and willing to listen to your children.

It's easy for us as men to get rigid in our ways and think that the way we do something is the right way. As an Empowered Father, you are encouraged to take a wider view. Assess yourself and find your strengths to build on and make any changes that need to happen. If you feel resistant to an idea, explore that resistance and see if it is trying to tell you something. Do not fear making mistakes because they are learning opportunities that will help you grow even stronger as a dad.

Let your parenting partner know what you have learned about yourself and keep them in the loop of what you continue to learn. If you are making changes, ask for their support and take their tips and observations in stride. Be open with yourself and with those around you that are part of your support network. A top priority of an Empowered Father is continually learning so you can make the changes necessary.

### "Someone's Got to Start the Change"

There is a story that sticks out to me about why fathers must not fear change, and it's the last one I want to leave with you before ending this book. It happened during a class I taught in a local jail for fathers. This particular group was mostly young fathers, about thirty-five and younger. Several were near the end of their sentence and excited to return to their lives and families soon. Others were not as close to the end of their sentence but still wanting ways to grow closer to their children. Among all these dads, in the back of the classroom, sat an older gentleman in his late sixties.

In the first few sessions, he did not speak much or write many notes down in his book. He was typically the last man into the classroom and the first to leave. However, I could tell through his body language that he never stopped watching or listening. From the front of the room, I could see that he was absorbing our discussion and thinking about it deeply.

In the final few session of the class, he began to speak up more. This man was the father of three children. He had lost one child to violence, another child had broken off contact with him nearly thirty years before, and his third son was still in touch and a father as well. He said he was scared to death to take the class because he believed he had failed as a dad already, having been incarcerated for more than half his life and most of his children's lives.

One of the fathers asked why he was taking this class, especially if his children were grown up and having families of their own. This was the first time I ever saw this man look down, almost as if he was hiding from the rest of us in the room. After a few deep breaths, he looked up with tears in his eyes and changed the lives of every man in that room, myself included.

The room was silent, and everyone's focus was on this

man. He told us that his youngest son was also incarcerated, following the horrible footsteps that he had left for him. Then came an even heavier bombshell. He continued, "that is not even the worst part. My grandson is also locked up in a juvenile detention center; that is my legacy as a father." Three generations of men in this family were currently incarcerated.

Out of genuine care and curiosity, another father asked what he hoped to get out of the class. With a few more tears falling from his eyes and a trembling voice, he responded with, "someone's got to start the change. I got us in this mess, I think I should get us out." This was a powerful moment that touched every person to the core.

This father's story taught me about the powerful impact we can have on our children, for the good or the bad. This man realized the legacy he was leaving for his son and grandson and wanted to take steps to change it. He hoped to change the course of his life, not for himself, but for those that followed him.

As fathers, we also have this same powerful impact on our children. At the beginning of this book, it was stated that you can change the world as a father. It is true! Empowered Fathers understand their power and seek to create a world that fosters growth and hope in their children. You control the legacy you leave behind for your children. If you had no father, you do not have to repeat that cycle. If your father was a hero to you, then you can choose to be a hero for your children.

This book challenged you to examine a lot about yourself. Some of it may have been tough, and other areas may have reinforced what you are currently doing. As you move forward in your journey, continue to be open, to challenge yourself, and to grow into the Empowered Father that you are! Consult this book as often as you need; it will always be here for you. If there are changes to be made, make them. Remember, "someone's got to start the change." Be the Empowered Father you are and change the world for your children! Be courageous, be humble, and never give up. I wish success to you and all of us that are on this journey of fatherhood together!

# | 13 |

# Thank You!

This book has been a labor of love, and I hope it has been what you were looking for. Drawing on all the experiences I have had working with fathers, teaching classes, forming programs, and being a father myself, have come together to create the Empowered Father concept. I am grateful that you have taken the challenge!

Your journey doesn't have to stop with the final pages of this book. There is always room for something more to learn. Empowered Fathering is a meaningful and transformational set of armor to put on for fathers, and your growth doesn't have to end here.

Continue your adventure with the Empowered Fathering: The Next Level Online Course. In this course you'll build on this book's concepts, learn new tips and ideas, and gain even more insight, and it is all accessible in the palm of your hand!

As a thank you for reading this book, enter the special code **EFBOOK20** for an **immediate 20% off** the Empowered Fathering: The Next Level Online Course. You can find it at courses.empoweringthejourney.com today!

Also, I always want to hear from you. I'd love to read the stories of what has changed, how things are different, and what your fatherhood journey looks like today. You can always provide me with feedback on what I can do better. All you need to do is send me an email at connect@empoweringthejourney.com to get ahold of me.

I look forward to it!

Congratulations, and get to building those relationships with your children!

Andrew Chris
Founder of The Life Empowerment Organization

# REFERENCES

**Sources:**

Appl, D. J., Brown, S., & Stone, M. (2008). A father's interactions with his toddler: Personal and professional lessons for early childhood educators. *Early Childhood Education Journal, 36*, 127-134.

Bauman, D. C., & Wasserman, K. B. (2010). Empowering fathers of disadvantaged preschoolers to take a more active role in preparing their children for literacy success at school. *Early Childhood Education Journal, 37*, 363-370.

Bretherton, I., Lamber, J. D., & Golby, B. (2005). Involved fathers of preschool children as seen by themselves and their wives: Accounts of attachment, socialization, and companionship. *Attachment & Human Development, 7*(3), 229-251.

Fatherhood Outcome Statistics retrieved from the National Fatherhood Initiative at www.fatherhood.org.

Long, E. C. J., Fish, J. N., Scheffler, A., & Hanert, B. (2014). Memorable experiences between fathers and sons: Stories that shape a son's identity and perspective of his father. *The Journal of Men's Studies, 22*(2), 122-139.

Luo, J., Wang, L-G., & Gao, W-B. (2011). The influence of the absence of fathers and the timing of separation on anxiety and self-esteem of adolescents: A cross-sectional survey. *Child: Care, Health and Development ,38,* 723-731.

Rohner, R. P., & Veneziana, R. A. (2001). The importance of father love: History and contemporary evidence. *Review of General Psychology, 5*(4), 382-405.

Rominov, H., Giallo, R., & Whelan, T. A. (2016). Father's postnatal distress, parenting self-efficacy, later parenting behavior, and children's emotional-behavioral functioning: A longitudinal study. *Journal of Family Psychology, 30*(8), 907-917.

Andrew Chris is the Founder of The Life Empowerment Organization LLC where he pursues his passion for empowering others and their relationships. Through extensive academic and professional experience in therapy, parent coaching, leadership, child development, and being a husband and father, he takes what he has learned and strives to change the lives of others for the positive.

Taking years of experience of working with thousands of different people, he takes hard to address problems in life and condenses them down to tangible and easy to use pieces of information. His core focus is on building relationships, especially the ones we have with ourselves, our partners, and our children.

With empowering resources that focus on the unique positives and strengths we all have within us, he seeks to change our lives and our world by affecting positive change in the ways we relate to ourselves and others.